scream free
PARENTING

screamfree
PARENTING

The Revolutionary Approach to
Raising Your Kids
Without
Losing Your Cool

HAL EDWARD RUNKEL, LMFT

BROADWAY BOOKS | NEW YORK

BROADWAY

PUBLISHED BY BROADWAY BOOKS

Copyright © 2007 by ScreamFree Omnimedia, LLC

All Rights Reserved

Published in the United States by Broadway Books,
an imprint of The Doubleday Broadway Publishing Group,
a division of Random House, Inc., New York.
www.broadwaybooks.com

BROADWAY BOOKS and its logo, a letter B bisected on the diagonal,
are trademarks of Random House, Inc.

Book design by Lisa Sloane

Library of Congress Cataloging-in-Publication Data
Runkel, Hal Edward.
   Screamfree parenting : the revolutionary approach to raising your kids
without losing your cool / Hal Edward Runkel. —1st ed.
      p. cm.
   1. Parenting. 2. Child rearing. 3. Discipline of children. I. Title.
II. Title: Screamfree parenting.

   HQ755.8.R86 2007
   649'.1—dc22

                                                         2006036516

ISBN 978-0-7679-2742-0

PRINTED IN THE UNITED STATES OF AMERICA

10 9 8 7 6 5 4 3 2 1

First Edition

To Jenny,
of course.

And to Hannah and to Brandon,
I'm thinking two things about you . . .

CONTENTS

ScreamFree™ \\'skrēm'frē\\: learning to relate with others in a calm, cool, and connected way, taking hold of your own emotional responses no matter how anyone else chooses to behave; learning to focus on yourself and take care of yourself for the world's benefit

How to Read This Book

My goal for this book is simple: *to calm the world, one relationship at a time*, beginning with your relationships with your kids. I firmly believe that by incorporating the principles outlined here into your way of life, you will begin to enjoy the types of parent-child relationships you have always craved. These are relationships full of joy, cooperation, harmony, and, most of all, mutual respect. Peace in your family is not as far off as you might think.

In order for this book to help you pursue such relationships, I have sought to provide a structure that logically introduces you to the ScreamFree way, one step at a time. At first, some of these principles may seem contrarian, even a bit heretical, for they run counter to a lot of popular teaching. So while you may feel tempted to skim the table of contents and skip forward to a topic that catches your eye, you will get the most out of the book by reading each chapter consecutively.

The book is divided into four parts, with multiple chapters in each. At the conclusion of each part, I tell a true story from the real-life experiences of real people just like you.

Some of these stories come from my coaching and/or therapy clients, some from colleagues and/or friends. I am honored and privileged to know and work with some of the most courageous people in the world, folks who choose to invest their time, money, and significant emotional energy in learning to focus on themselves and the way they relate with others. Walking alongside them and watching them revolutionize their relationships in the process is my undeserved blessing.

In each of these stories you will see the power of Scream-Free Parenting in action. Of course, the names and details have been altered to protect confidentiality, but the events are all true—and powerful. I have selected each of these stories because they wonderfully illustrate the principles of the preceding section. As you will see, these stories represent parent-child relationships in various stages of life. While everyone's story is different, I know you can find yourself in here somewhere.

Above all, take from this book whatever inspires you to revolutionize your relationships and discard the rest. You do not have to accept all that I say in order to enjoy the types of relationships you crave or become the type of parent you desire to be.

All you have to do, you will see, is learn to keep your cool.

Please e-mail me at feedback@screamfree.com, and let me know how this book intersects with your life. I look forward to hearing from you about your journey with Scream-Free Parenting. Your feedback helps provide the inspiration I use to continue on this journey to calm the world.

PART ONE

Becoming the "Cool" Parent Your Kids Really Need

Parents can tell but never teach, unless they
practice what they preach.
—ARNOLD H. GLASGOW, PSYCHOLOGIST

In raising my children, I have lost my mind
but found my soul.
—LISA T. SHEPHERD, PARENT

Every kid wants to have "cool" parents. No, this does
not mean kids want parents who try to be hip to the
latest styles (that makes you decidedly uncool). And
contrary to some popular teaching, being a cool parent does
not mean being so permissive that you let your kids do
whatever they want. What every kid wants are parents who
can *keep their cool*, even when things get hot. *Especially* when

things get hot. Kids want parents who are far less anxious and far more levelheaded than they are. Your kids want you to remain unflappable, even when they flip out.

As it turns out, that's exactly what they need.

Parents everywhere are facing the toughest challenge of their lives: trying to create a loving family environment filled with mutual respect and cooperation. And they're trying to do this in a culture that celebrates irresponsibility and self-indulgence. It's no wonder parents feel more anxious than ever before. They feel overwhelmed and underappreciated. And I believe they all want help.

I believe parents are searching for someone to present an inspiring vision of how it all could be different.

Parents are searching for someone to present an inspiring vision of how it all could be different. We have heard all sorts of packaged programs delivering fail-proof techniques to raise perfect children. We've heard about the countless failures of the past two generations while at the same time hearing of the urgent need to return to the good ol' days. And most of all, we have been bombarded with the call to sacrifice ourselves for the sake of our kids, focus all of our attention on what our kids need, and learn to always be there for them.

We've heard all of this and more, and it's not helping. This call for total self-sacrifice is actually hurting, leaving parents feeling more overwhelmed, more frustrated, and less capable.

So, what's wrong? Or better yet, what's the right direction out of this mess? A few years ago, a brilliant family therapist and rabbi named Edwin Friedman asked a critical question: When's the last time you saw a parenting book telling parents to focus *less* on their children?[1]

Well, this may be the first one you've ever seen. *Scream-Free Parenting* may be the first book you've read that tells all parents to stop orbiting their lives around their children and return the focus to themselves.

So is that the problem, that we're too focused on our kids? Absolutely. In a rash reaction to the children-should-be-seen-and-not-heard formula that many of our parents grew up with, we have gone to another extreme, the our-lives-revolve-around-our-children formula. Just look at us chauffeuring our kids from school, to practice, to yet another practice in a minivan with stickers plastered all over it. And whose name is on these stickers? Whose name is emblazoned on this minivan that we paid for? Whether it be an honor student badge or a soccer ball, our kids' names tell the whole world who really owns the vehicle. And our lives. And it's not good for them or us.

ScreamFree Parenting provides a way out of this mess, a way to restore both parent and child to their rightful places in the home.

Why ScreamFree?

Not all of us scream at our kids. Not all of us struggle with keeping our cool. But all parents do experience, to various levels or degrees, a universal struggle. We all feel incredibly anxious about our kids, and their choices, and we don't know what to do about it. We fret and worry about how our kids will turn out. Inevitably, we're so focused on our kids that we don't realize when this anxiety takes over—and we get reactive.

ScreamFree Parenting is about calming all of our reactive responses to this anxiety. It's called ScreamFree because screaming is the most popular reaction. But there are other reactions, such as disconnecting ourselves from the situation. Or beginning to overcompensate (ever pick up after your kids because you're so tired of battling them about it?). Some of us just give up . . . and keep giving in.

All of these reactions are just different ways of "screaming." And they are all just as ineffective in creating the type of relationships we crave with our children. But there is hope. There *is* a better way.

What I offer in this book is a way for you to envision yourself in a nonreactive, yet fully connected, relationship with each of your children. And that's the catch—remaining both calm *and* connected. Many parents can remain calm by simply disengaging from the relationship. Other parents stay fully engaged, only to let their anxiety drive the relationship. *ScreamFree Parenting* teaches you to calm your own anxiety first, enabling you to remain fully connected and involved. And this creates a revolutionary relationship with each of your kids and the rest of your family—a relationship where your position is that of an inspiring influence; a relationship where your number-one leadership role in the family is that of a calming authority. Regardless of the ages of your children and regardless of the mistakes you've made up to this point, you can restore yourself to this position in the family.

**Your number-one leadership role in the family
is that of a *calming authority*.**

You can—by learning to focus on yourself, calm yourself down, and grow yourself up—begin to make changes in the way you parent, changes that dramatically change the dynamics of your family. You can, beginning today, start practicing the principles that will bring about new patterns of connection and cooperation. Such changes won't be easy, and they won't come automatically. Becoming a Scream-Free Parent involves a difficult journey, facing difficult truths about yourself and your relationships. Difficult, but not impossible. But it's not all tough stuff either—becoming a ScreamFree Parent also invites you to treat yourself better than you've ever thought you could or should.

It all begins with one fundamental shift. As you will see, parenting is not about children, it's about parents.

CHAPTER ONE

Parenting Is Not About Kids, It's About Parents

It's not you, it's me.
—George Costanza, *Seinfeld*

The greatest thing you can do for your kids is learn to focus on yourself.

That statement might not make complete sense right now. It might, in fact, seem downright offensive. What? Turn the focus away from my children and onto myself? Isn't that against all the rules?

No, it isn't. I'm not proposing that you put your children last on the list. Far from it. What I am saying is that by focusing on yourself, you will have a healthier, happier relationship with your whole family.

You see, most of us have been operating with a faulty model of how to live in our relationships. That's not to say our relationships are all faulty, but the model sure is. We've been operating with a model that says in order to have healthy relationships, we need to focus on meeting other people's needs, trying to serve them and make them happy. To even question such a model draws controversy, I know, but stay with me.

By focusing on yourself, you will have a healthier, happier relationship with your whole family.

This book is going to talk about why this model is so faulty, particularly in our parent-child relationships. For now, there are a few simple things we should consider. First, it's a given that there are things in this world we can control and things we cannot control. Now ask yourself this question: How smart is it to focus your energy on something you can't do anything about, something you cannot control? Answer: Not very. Follow-up question: Which category do your kids fall into? In other words, are your children something you can control or something you cannot control? Here's an even tougher question: Even if you could control your kids, should you? Is that what parenting is all about? And what if it's not the kids who are out of control?

Who's Really Out of Control Here?

My kids, Hannah and Brandon, were four and two, and it was one of *those* Saturday mornings. My wife, Jenny, and I had stayed up way too late on Friday night, which guaranteed that our kids would get up way too early the next day. And so the weekend began with a lot of whining and crying and complaining—and the kids were upset as well.

So I decided, in my parenting expert wisdom, to get us all out of the house. Let's go to Waffle House for breakfast. Now the first Waffle House we walked into was just too full, but, thankfully, there is no shortage of Waffle Houses in suburban Atlanta. So, we piled back into the car, strapped our children into their car seats, quieted disappointed whines with promises of lots of maple syrup, and drove the hundred yards or so to a second Waffle House. And the line at the second one was just as long as the first.

There was no way we were getting the kids back into the car for another trip, however, so we decided to wait it out. Thankfully, the staff at this Waffle House were thinking—they had crayons and blank paper for the kids. My wife and I could even get in a little adult conversation. A win-win situation.

As if that weren't enough, a sign caught my eye. If my children drew a picture, they were entitled to a paper Waffle House hat—just like the grill man wears—and a free waffle. Sometimes life is good. The kids colored. My wife and I talked. The time flew and before we knew it, we were seated—my wife and daughter on one side of the booth, my son and I on the other. They brought the kids their paper hats, and I even tried one on.

If you've never been to a Waffle House, you would be amazed at the consistency of their architecture. All the tables surround the kitchen, and wall-length windows surround the tables. It's very open, and it's easy to notice the goings-on of others.

Now, while I was feeling pretty good by this time, my kids hadn't eaten anything all morning. Hungry kids who've done nothing but wait around can be . . . restless. Hannah, our four-year-old, handled it all right, just garden-variety complaints. But Brandon, our two-year-old, sure was feeling two years old, if you know what I mean. Two-year-olds generally have no regard for things like "practicing an inside voice" or "using words like a big boy" when they've been forced in and out of a car with nothing to eat but promises. Cooperating with me was not high on his list of priorities at the time. Enjoying a nice family breakfast didn't seem like such a good idea now.

But I'm a Licensed Marriage and Family Therapist. I'm a relationship coach. I know how to control myself and keep from losing my temper. I know better than to react and resort to yelling and violent acts of coercion. I can stay calm in the face of increasing levels of anxiety. But then my son threw his fork on the floor. My resolve began to fade.

The fork made a loud noise, causing all the people around us to look at me. Some of them even pointed and whispered (at least that's what it felt like they were doing). I looked over at my perfect wife sitting there with my perfect daughter. There is an unwritten rule among parents with multiple kids: Whoever is sitting on your side is on your watch. So while the women in my life are enjoying this angelic scene of cooperation and intimacy, my son and I are on the verge of World War III.

Nothing is making him happy, nothing is stopping him

from the beginning stages of an all-out tantrum. Finally, his waffle arrives and I think the battle will be over soon. So, I start to cut the waffle up, but he doesn't want the waffle cut up. Maybe he wants to eat the whole thing with his hands in one bite, I don't know. I do know I'm feeling closer and closer to my own emotional edge.

But I'm the expert on human relationships, right? I'm the one planning to write a book someday called *ScreamFree Parenting*. Was I going to allow a two-year-old to push my buttons? You bet I was. See, the fork got such a great response, my son began to wonder what might happen if he threw his waffle—plate and all—on the floor.

Here's what might happen: Daddy might lose his cool! And that's precisely what did happen.

I hastily apologized to the people with syrup splatter on their feet and then snatched Brandon out of his booster seat. Then I apologized to the man sitting in the booth behind us after Brandon's foot hit him in the back of the head. And then we stormed out of the restaurant. All eyes were fixed on us as my son kept screaming. And kicking. And hitting. I was seething as I pushed the door open with such force that it rattled the glass walls. The reverberating structure got everyone's attention. The entire restaurant saw me outside on the sidewalk, yelling at my son, using big words, asking rhetorical questions, puffing out my chest, pointing my finger, and intimidating a boy who couldn't have stood more than thirty-six inches tall. What a big man I was!

Finally, somehow, the ugly scene ended. Brandon and I returned to our seats to complete our nice family breakfast. And there sat Jenny, my loving and faithful wife. I think she wanted to say something supportive and reassuring, but she just couldn't contain the smirk. I was a volcano looking for an excuse to erupt.

"What?" I barked.

"Nice hat."

It was then that I realized the paper Waffle House hat still sat squarely on top of my head. The entire scene had taken place with a silly hat on top of a silly man who wanted nothing more than to be taken seriously.

Our Biggest Enemy as Parents

Truth be told, I didn't need the hat to make me look foolish. I had done that myself with my knee-jerk reactivity. In fact, that kind of emotional reaction is our worst enemy when it comes to having great relationships.

Let me say that again: *Emotional reactivity is our worst enemy when it comes to having great relationships.*

If you don't get anything else from this book, get this: Our biggest struggle as parents is not with the television; it's not with bad influences; it's not even with drugs or alcohol. Our biggest struggle as parents is with our own emotional reactivity. That's why the greatest thing we can do for our kids is learn to focus on us, not them. Instead of anxiously trying to control our kids, let's concentrate on what we can control—calming our own emotional, knee-jerk reactions.

What's so damaging about being too reactive? Keep reading. The next couple of chapters will make it clear. For now, consider this: How can we have any influence on our children's decision-making if we don't have an influence on our own? When we get reactive, we get regressive. That is, we shrink back to an immature level of functioning. Think of me at Waffle House. In an effort to get my two-year-old to stop acting so immaturely, I became just as immature.

How effective can that be? I've come to realize that if I get loud and scary and intimidating, I may get compliance eventually, but at what price? I may have screamed my son into submission at Waffle House, but what type of relationship will I have with him if I continue to parent by reactive intimidation?

If we want to be influential, then we have to first bring ourselves under control. Only then can we choose our response. Only then can we choose how we want to behave, regardless of how our children choose to behave.

So if emotional reactivity is our biggest enemy, where does it come from? More important, what can we do about it? Most of us cannot think of a more terrifying emotion than feeling overwhelmed. We can feel scared, exhausted, worried, or angry, but nothing shuts us down, stops us in our tracks, and causes us to throw up our hands in futility like feeling overwhelmed. When we feel incapable of coping with, handling, or accomplishing all we have to do, we are overwhelmed. When it seems as if even if we weren't so tired and so frustrated we still couldn't keep all the plates spinning, that's about as scary as it gets. When we feel stretched beyond our limits, that's when we just want to quit.

And I can think of no more accurate description of how most of us parents feel far too much of the time. Far too often, we feel overwhelmed. We feel overstretched, overcommitted, underprepared, and underappreciated. That's a recipe for feeling overwhelmed. As a result, most of us feel a gnawing sense of inadequacy. We don't just feel like bad parents, we feel like failures.

Parents feel overstretched, overcommitted, underprepared, and underappreciated.

And unfortunately, our role as parents is the one area of life where we cannot afford to fail. If there is one area where we feel the pressure of absolute success, it is with our parenting. After all, we are bombarded with messages about the importance of time with our kids, involvement in our kids' lives, and putting our family first among our priorities. Magazines are crammed with articles dispensing the newest parenting techniques and advice. Studies consistently show the ill effects of bad parenting. Churches preach the need to put families first. With all of this pressure comes just more fear and feelings of inadequacy.

And then there's the most intense pressure of all: How we do as parents will reverberate throughout history. We are raising the next generation, and they will either continue the success and progress of past generations or they will erase it all.

Anyone feeling overwhelmed?

Parenting is serious business. The stakes are unbelievably high. The cost of failure is unimaginable. I know you feel the intense weight of performing as a parent. You may wonder if you're the only one who sometimes feels inadequate, even inept. You may wonder: Is it supposed to be this hard? The answer is yes. And no. Yes, parenting is hard, and it's supposed to be. We'll get to that in the next few chapters. But no, we don't have to feel this much pressure. We don't have to feel overwhelmed.

The Most Damaging Lie About Parenting

The reason we feel so overwhelmed is because most of us are attempting to follow an impossible model. And it is fueled by a dangerous lie. Here is the most damaging lie about parenting: We are responsible *for* our children.

I know that to even question such a statement sounds ridiculous. "Of course I'm responsible for my kids . . . who else would be?" I can only ask you to bear with me and keep reading.

You see, most people would define parenting like this: "It is our job as parents to get our children to think, feel, and, especially, behave the right way. It is our job to get our children to be good." Of course that's right, right?

Wrong.

Now, let me be clear. In my experience working with families, I've seen the devastating effects of terrible parenting on now-grown adults. Certainly we have a profound amount of influence on how our kids turn out. This book will illustrate the power we have to shape our children. In fact, I don't think we can overestimate this influence we have on future generations.

But what that really means is that we have a far greater responsibility *to* our children than we have *for* our children. Let me say that again, so it will sink in. We are much less responsible *for* our children than we've ever been told.

However, we have a far greater responsibility *to* our children than we've ever realized.

Most of us feel like we're responsible *for* our children. Sure, they're totally dependent on us right from the beginning. But let's think about that for a moment. If we are responsible *for* our children, then we have a really big problem. How long did it take you to realize that your child had a mind of her own? Early on, our children start to make their own choices. This is part of growing up. In truth, this *is* growing up. Even in infancy our kids start to embrace their natural ability to make decisions about what they will and will not do. They begin to choose how they feel, how they think, and how they behave.

I know this concept is simplistic, but it carries all the seeds of our frustration in raising kids. They simply make different choices than we want them to make! They choose to yell and scream in the grocery store. They choose not to do their homework. They choose to break curfew and disrespect our rules. They choose to throw their waffles on the floor in front of a restaurant full of people!

If you are responsible *for* your children, then you have to figure out how to program them to make the "right" choices. And you need to do it quickly. You have to learn the right techniques to get them to think, feel, and behave according to your definition of "good."

All of this sounds alarmingly like obedience training. It comes as no surprise, then, to find parenting books at your local bookseller written by animal trainers. "What works for Fido can work for your child!"

If you're totally responsible for coercing your children into being good, then it makes perfect sense to enlist some program or system like that. Such an approach may make parents feel big and in charge, but it leaves children feeling small and incompetent.

The fact that our children have been given the power of choice, as self-directed human beings, can thwart even the best obedience-training program. Children will soon realize they are in a no-win situation. Either they kill their own decision-making spirit in an attempt to reduce their parents' anxiety, or they rebel against their parents' authority. That's the catch-22 of the "responsible *for*" model of parenting. Parents either program their children correctly or they have failed. Children either conform to the system, surrender their individuality, and become "the child we don't have to worry about," or they rebel against the system, failing to "get with the program."

Do you see the two categories we have neatly set up? On one hand, we have "What Will Make Mom and Dad Less Anxious," and on the other hand, we have "Wrong Choices That Will Make Mom and Dad More Anxious." For most families, there simply is no third option. In this system, the possibility of children learning to act for themselves and think critically about their choices does not exist. Doing so would equal rebellion. If your child ends up "doing the right thing," then you've raised a robot. He did exactly as he was programmed to do. But if your child ends up thinking and acting for himself, then you've raised a rebel.

There *Is* a Better Way

But there has to be another way—a way to say yes to our profound influence on our children's lives without taking total responsibility *for* those lives. There must be a way to dramatically influence the life of a child without resorting to programming and coercion. I call this third option Scream-Free Parenting, because it emphasizes a radical focus on and approach to calming our own anxiety.

Again, not all of us scream at our children, but all of us struggle with reactive behaviors. We may scream, we may manipulate, we may even use violence. Or we may neglect, we may avoid, we may even withhold love. These are all different examples of emotional reactivity. As I said before, they are all just different ways of screaming. ScreamFree Parenting takes all of this reactivity incredibly seriously and says *the only way to retain a position of influence with our children is to regain a position of control over ourselves.*

Initially, this type of intense self-focus may sound too selfish. Or even misguided. "I need a book to help me get *my kids* to behave, not me!" you might protest. I promise that if you stick with me through the first part of this book, you will see that it is all designed to make you far less selfish, far more mature, and far more capable as a parent. Capable of the type of influence your kids really need from you. For now, the bottom line is this: You need to be in control of the things you can control, and that starts (and may end) with you.

You're responsible *to* your children, your spouse, your friends, and family members. You're accountable to them for how you think, feel, and behave toward them.

> The only way to retain a position of influence
> with our children is to regain a position of
> control over ourselves.

I want you to actually say this out loud: "I am responsible *to* my child for how I behave, regardless of how he or she behaves."

Again, the focus is on you because ultimately you are the only one you can control. If you make sure you behave—even when your kids misbehave—then you have a greater chance of positively influencing the situation, any situation. That is ScreamFree Parenting.

In this book you'll read several stories of parents facing the very situations you face. They range from the ordinary, such as the bedtime struggles with a toddler, to the dramatic, such as the Mom-I-just-got-into-a-wreck scenario we all dread. All these situations create anxiety, sometimes the intense, I-don't know-if-I-can-handle-this type of anxiety. And that's okay.

This book will help you face similar situations, whether your kids are tots or teenagers, with a renewed confidence in your own integrity. Becoming a ScreamFree Parent involves a growing self-awareness, a greater sense of self-direction, and an increased willingness to take personal responsibility for your actions, regardless of the actions of those around you.

Come to think of it, isn't that what we want for our kids? We want them to be self-aware, self-directed, and able to take personal responsibility for their actions. But they will never get there if we don't model it all for them. You see, this parenting stuff is more about us than it is about them.

The first idea in this book is: The greatest thing you can do for your kids is learn to focus on yourself. Getting rid of the weight of the responsible-*for* model is the first step. In the rest of the book, we turn our focus toward all that's involved in your responsibility *to* your children.

This will not be an easy journey. Once you turn the focus inward, you always learn more about yourself than you want to know. Like how easily you allow access to your emotional buttons, hoping others "just don't go there." Or how much you've been trying to teach your children lessons you have yet to learn yourself. Turning your attention to yourself is not a self-indulgent journey. On the contrary, it is all about discovering where you still need to grow. And that's what becoming ScreamFree is all about—opening your eyes to your own continued maturity so you can lead your kids toward theirs.

I would tell you to hold on to your hat, because it's going to be a bumpy ride. But then again, the last thing we need to do is keep wearing our silly hats.

Reflection Questions

1. The opening line of this chapter is "The greatest thing you can do for your kids is learn to focus on yourself." When you read that line for the first time, what was your initial reaction?

2. Is your reaction any different now that you've read the chapter?

3. Recall one of the times you have felt your children were out of control. If you had had greater control over your own emotions, how could the situation have had a different outcome?

4. In the past, what has prevented you from focusing on yourself? Was it fear of being self-centered? Fear of finding out things you didn't want to know about yourself? Fear of blaming yourself for everything and letting others off the hook?

5. What do you think are your responsibilities *to* each of your children?

CHAPTER TWO

If You're Not Under Control,
Then You Cannot Be in Charge

Please don't make me angry.
You wouldn't like me when I'm angry.
—Bruce Banner (aka The Incredible Hulk)

Despite the success of the feature film *Hulk* released in 2003, my favorite adaptation of the Incredible Hulk comic book character goes back to the campy television version of the 1970s. An old photo of a young, skinny kid, painted green from head to toe for Halloween, proves my early devotion.

In many ways, the Hulk was the anti-superhero. Bruce Banner may have been the mild-mannered alter ego, but when he got mad, we weren't always sure the green monster was going to act for good. He didn't have a spot on the

Justice League, that's for sure. Comics freaks might think of him as one of the original X-Men, a mutant, forever changed by an unfortunate mishap and forever longing to return to normal.

What made the show compelling was the struggle we watched week after week. This nice, peaceful man tried in vain to contain the raging monster lurking just below the surface. We never knew what it was going to take to set him off, but we knew that at least once in each show he would be transformed and all hell would break loose. Perhaps what was most frustrating for Bruce Banner was that he wasn't fully aware of what the Hulk would do or had done. He was only aware of what he was *capable* of doing.

That's why the famous quote was so poignant: "Please don't make me angry. You wouldn't like me when I'm angry."

He didn't like himself when he was angry.

Bruce Banner could not control the reactive monster within. The control he needed to manage his condition was always in the hands of everyone else. That's why he had to warn the people around him. It was up to them to manage his reactions, because he had lost the ability to control himself. And the results were not pretty. In fact, they were usually disastrous.

It's one thing to believe you're The Incredible Hulk when you're seven years old and it's Halloween; that's cute. It's another thing to believe it when you're a grown man having lunch in a public place with your wife and kids; that's sad.

I recently watched a man take his family hostage. He sat there with his wife, his ten-year-old son, and a toddler in a high chair. No one talked. The family looked like they had been muzzled, not allowed to make eye contact or interact at all. When the mom started to feed the toddler, I found out why.

After a couple of fussy refusals to open his mouth, the father shouted at the child, "Eat!" There was no pretense of propriety, no understanding that we were all in a public place, an enclosed space. There was only a disrespectful bark.

Later the older son started blowing bubbles in his drink. This time the father actually screamed these words: "You're about to push me past my breaking point!" It's hard to believe a ten-year-old has that much power, that he can push a grown man past his breaking point.

"Don't make me angry. You wouldn't like me when I'm angry."

The unfortunate truth is that many of us live our relationships this way. We continually surrender control over our emotional responses to those around us. When we need others to accept us or validate us by doing whatever we tell them to do, we make them the caretakers of our emotional remote controls.

We continually surrender control over our emotional responses to those around us.

Bonzi Wells, a guy who gets paid to play basketball for the NBA, was once fined for making an obscene gesture at a fan. When questioned later about the incident, he responded, "If that fan was a little more professional, you know, I probably wouldn't have had to do that."

Okay, who's getting paid to be there? Who's supposed to be the professional? Please.

Of course, we can't judge Bonzi too harshly. We've all been guilty of pinning our emotional responses on others. According to the Hebrew Bible, it all started back in the Garden of Eden with Adam and Eve. After they ate the forbidden fruit, they started the blame game. First Adam blames Eve, then he blames God for creating Eve in the first place. Eve then blames the serpent. It's no wonder one of their sons killed the other in a jealous, reactive rage; reactive, other-focused patterns don't fall far from the tree.

Whatever you believe about the story, it demonstrates one solid truth: We've been blaming others from the very beginning.

Your emotional responses are up to you.
You always have a choice.

Taking responsibility for your own actions is a sign of maturity. Owning up to your mistakes without blaming your circumstances, other people, or your childhood—this is when you know you're a grown-up. But that's only one step on the path to bringing yourself "under control."

Learning to be "under control" means taking responsibility for your decisions before, during, and after you make them. I am not saying you don't ever make mistakes; this isn't about trying to be flawless. This is recognizing that no one, not even your kids, can *make* you feel anything, think anything, or do anything. Period. Your children cannot push you over the edge, press your magic buttons, or bring you to the brink. They are simply not that powerful.

Your emotional responses are up to you. You always have a choice.

If You Live by the Remote,
You Die by the Remote

You may have seen the commercial where a man is shown watching television, remote control in hand, as his wife enters the room. When he asks what's for dinner, she begins a lengthy monologue on this little dress she's been wanting. The exasperated husband aims the remote at his wife, pushes the fast-forward button, and suddenly she speeds up. He keeps the button pressed until he finally hears "Turkey potpie!" The commercial ends with the woman holding the remote. Her husband is sneaking out the back door, golf clubs in hand, when she points the remote at him. She pushes the button to change his channel, and suddenly, much to his surprise, he puts his clubs down and starts doing laundry.

We laugh at this commercial because it reflects a deep fantasy for us all: getting other people to do what we want, when we want, the way we want. Like the Adam Sandler character in *Click*, we often cherish the thought of having a remote control, sending automated commands toward our coworkers, our spouse, and, especially, our kids. Wouldn't that be wonderful? Push a button, any button:

"Go to bed without arguing."

"Do your homework."

"Quit hitting your sister."

"Take no for an answer."

"Become a well-adjusted, self-directed adult."

Here's the problem: When it comes to relationships, you can only hold one remote control at a time. When you grab for someone else's remote, you automatically give him or her access to your own. Don't believe me? What happens when you tell your daughter to pick up after herself and she says no? All she has to do is exert her own choice, a choice not to obey your command, and everything changes. Now she has begun pushing your buttons. Now you're locked in a button-pushing contest. Maybe you get louder or more intimidating. Maybe she gets more belligerent, more defiant. Very common. Not very productive.

If you live by the remote, you die by the remote. If you come to rely on your ability to control others, you are destined for frustration and misery. All they have to do is say no, and you're beside yourself. You're out of control, because you're trying to control something you have no business controlling.

What Does It Mean to Be "In Charge"?

Being "in charge" as a ScreamFree Parent is a fundamental shift in your objective as a parent. To truly be in charge means having the power to create lasting and continued growth, not just exerting power or demanding obedience. It means inspiring your children to motivate themselves.

I'll say that again: *To be "in charge" as a parent means inspiring your children to motivate themselves.*

This makes for a radical shift, a shift from controlling your kids' behavior to influencing their decisions. Your goal is not to control. Your goal is to influence. Remember, you are not responsible *for* your children's responses. You want to continually hold up and respect their ability to make choices, even choices you disagree with. Unless they're free to make their own choices, they can't learn the connection between choices and consequences. We'll talk more about this later, but for now, focus on the paradigm shift you have to make: You should not be in the business of forcing compliance at all costs. That kind of parenting only works over the short term and sows the seeds for long-term disaster. We may not like to hear that, but it's true.

When we try to force our children to comply with our sometimes unreasonable demands, we turn parenting into warfare. We even use warfare terminology: "You've got to pick your battles." I'd like parents to eliminate that phrase from their rhetoric, because language has an amazing ability to frame interactions. If I think of my interactions with my children as a series of battles, I cannot help but go into the situation expecting a fight.

In his book *Raising Children You Can Live With*, family therapist Jaime Raser says this: "Parenting is not a series of 'techniques' or 'manipulations' designed to gain control over another human being. It is a special kind of relationship between a parent and a child."

Later in the same book Raser says:

Children can draw parents into interactions that become Us (the children) against Them (authority figures), not Us against the realistic and logical consequences of rules. Us against Them becomes a war. "Getting tougher" can win battles, but it may also teach that winning is the most important goal and that force and power are the ways to win. Children then learn that, with enough power, they can also win and that this is how the world operates. If they feel they are losing, they simply apply more power.[1]

This battle can seem endless, and that's because it is. There are no victors in relationship battles, just more casualties. When you need your children to comply for your sake, you're creating a power-based exchange that asks them to be the caretakers of your emotional state.

There are no victors in relationship battles, just more casualties.

What We're Really Screaming

We've all heard that there is more to communication than just words. What comes out of our mouths makes up only a small part of what actually gets communicated. The content of any communication is not nearly as important as the context.

When we scream at our kids, when we get emotionally reactive, we communicate one single message: CALM ME DOWN! No matter what words are actually coming out of our mouths, no matter how long our tirade is, no matter how old our children are, when we scream, the message is always the same: CALM ME DOWN! Whenever we react to our children's behavior by screaming, we are actually begging them to help us calm our anxiety.

We are saying that we just cannot handle the fact they

will not obey or listen or calm down. We cannot handle this, so we flip out.

"I CANNOT BELIEVE YOU DID THIS!"

"WHAT IN THE WORLD WERE YOU THINKING?"

"LOOK AT ME WHEN I TALK TO YOU!"

Insert whatever words you want; the message is always the same: "I need you to comply or else I'm going to lose it. And when I lose it, I'm going to need you to comply so I can calm back down. All my emotional responses are up to you."

How is a four-year-old or a fourteen-year-old supposed to deal with that much pressure? And that's what it is, pressure. When we put all our emotional buttons in children's hands, we become totally focused on them. We have begun a sort of orbit around them, attaching all of our emotional responses to how they perform in school, whether they use good manners, or whatever other choices they're making today. The entire family's emotional life is now tied to the whims, frailties, and growing pains of the least mature members of the family.

"Calm me down, son, because I cannot calm myself."

It doesn't sound much different from Bruce Banner.

So what can you do differently?

You can take back your remote control. You have to make holding your own emotional responses in your own hands your number-one priority.

Calming Yourself Down

"That *sounds* great," you say. "But in the heat of the moment, it seems I'm more inclined to do exactly the opposite."

I know. In the blurry messiness that makes for an anxious moment, we start to rush, we start to panic, and we start to focus on the other person. We all have triggers—certain sights, sounds, or words that set us off or shut us down. Our triggers can vary in intensity, depending on the time of day, or the person we're dealing with, or the location of the situation. And it definitely seems that no one sets us off quite like our kids.

"I hate you!"

"You're stupid!"

"Mommy, I made an accident in the kitchen."

"She hit me!"

"I wish I had a different daddy."

"I never get to do anything! It's not fair!"

"Why do you always have to go to work?"

"I got my report card today."

"Dad, I just got in a wreck."

"Mom, I think I might be pregnant."

Whoa! That got intense at the end, didn't it? As parenting expert Dr. James Dobson so appropriately titled one of his books, *Parenting Isn't for Cowards.*

Steve Martin has a great scene in the film *Bringing Down the House.* Upon the advice of his hip and streetwise new friend (played by Queen Latifah), Steve's character decides to approach his teenage daughter—who's just stumbled in after an all-nighter—with calm instead of rage. With the facial contortions that only Steve Martin can create, we watch his attempts to stay smiling, cool, and calm on the outside while clearly doing a white-knuckled boil-over on the inside. The results are even better than he expected.

After his daughter told him things that happened at the party—more shocking details than he really wanted to know—she was so happy he didn't blow up, she threw her arms around his neck and exclaimed, "Oh, Daddy! I'm so happy to be able to talk to you! There is so much more that I want to tell you!"

Of course, that's just a movie and things don't happen like that in real life, right?

Wrong. I've seen that type of connection hundreds of times, especially with teenagers, once parents learned to control their reactions.

But let's take the same scene and play it differently, this time without the self-control.

Let's say Martin's character reacts more like, well, like any of us might if we weren't working hard at it. What do you think would happen if a daughter came in after being out all night and the father had neither the desire nor the ability to calm his reactivity?

I'm going to take a leap and say he would lose complete control of himself and hit the ceiling. Given that reaction, how much closer do you think the two would become by the end of the ensuing screaming match? What would happen to that father's ability to influence the situation? Where would his authority go at that point? Out the window, just like his daughter would if he kept reacting that way.

Giving in to your reactivity actually helps create the very

outcomes you're trying to avoid. This is because of a process called anxiety transfer. We've just looked at two different reactions to an identical situation. In the first scene, the father calmed himself down and, as a result, his daughter became calmer—calm enough to trust him and confide in him. She reacted to his calming influence, and the result was a more trusting relationship.

In the second scene, we imagined the father allowing his anxiety to get the better of him. He blew up and hit the ceiling. His anxiety over his inability to control his daughter and his fear for her safety then got transferred over to her. Her reaction, therefore, became defensive. A screaming match ensued. And the result was the further crippling of the relationship.

Now, many of you might be saying she deserved whatever she got because she committed such a horrible offense, staying out all night. I am not saying that choices to break the rules need go undisciplined. I am not saying that in order to foster a calm and trusting relationship, you need to let your kids go without discipline. Nothing could be further from the truth.

But for you to exercise a position of authority in your family, for you to have the lasting influence on your child's choices you so desperately crave, you have to first calm down. You have to calm your own anxiety, refusing to transfer it over to your child and make any situation worse.

In order to be in charge, you have to bring yourself under control.

Reflection Questions

1. What situation with your child seems to make you the most reactive?

2. What is your typical way of screaming?

3. When you lose your temper, who are you usually tempted to blame?

4. Has anyone ever tried to make you lose your temper on purpose? How did you respond?

5. Recall a time when you were proud of the fact that you remained calm and connected during a heated situation. How did your calm presence affect the outcome?

CHAPTER THREE

Growing Up Is Hard to Do, Especially for Grown-ups

Nobody said it was easy;
No one ever said it would be this hard.
—COLDPLAY, "THE SCIENTIST"

Child-rearing myth: Labor ends when the baby is born.
—UNKNOWN

I have always hated the phrase "No pain, no gain."

Actually, I've only hated it when someone else has said it to me. That's because it's rarely said in a nurturing and hopeful sort of way. It usually means "Stop your whining!" I usually hear it when I'm under a barbell at the gym, wondering if my insurance covers exercise accidents.

I actually like "No pain, no gain" when I get to say it to someone else, such as my wife or my buddies or my kids.

That way I get to be the one standing above them, dispensing from on high the wisdom I've accumulated through my years of personal struggle. I get to relish watching all the "productive" pain they now have to endure.

The truth is, "No pain, no gain" has a lot of truth to it. Pain is often the greatest catalyst to powerful change. Think of the way we build muscle. By intentionally inducing strain and tension in a controlled environment, we add size, strength, and endurance. But there is a catch to the saying's truth and effectiveness. The saying is only true—it only has actual power to change our lives—when we can say it to ourselves. A coach, a teacher, a personal trainer, or even an author can say it and believe it, but until we incorporate it into our core beliefs, into our very bones, it will do nothing but frustrate us. It's only when we say it, repeat it, and believe it ourselves that it becomes a true catalyst for change.

**Pain is often the greatest catalyst
to powerful change.**

That's what makes this chapter so challenging for me to write and, very possibly, for you to read. If I wrote this as if I were your personal family guru doling out wisdom from some mountaintop, I'd leave you with nothing but a handful of pithy sayings. I would have failed to teach you anything about your life and your parenting. The only way for this to work is for our conversation to inspire you to inspire yourself. And that can only happen if we tell the truth.

First, let us reaffirm what you already know about being

a parent: It's probably the most challenging thing you've ever done. Let us also reaffirm, however, what you hope about being a parent: It can be among the most rewarding experiences you've ever imagined.

So, we have a good news–bad news scenario. The bad news is that parenting is hard. Nothing you learn in this book will make that go away. The good news is that parenting is rewarding. No pain, no gain. But reading the good news here won't make it become a reality until you're ready to believe it and act on it.

Growing Pains

Parenting is painful at times, and you already know it's really difficult. But what you might not know is that parenting is supposed to be that way. Why? Parenting is a growth process, that's why. And nothing has ever grown without feeling some sort of growing pains. A saying attributed to Jesus takes this even further: No seed can bear fruit unless it first dies in the ground. No wonder it feels like this parenting thing is gonna kill us!

In many ways, you have already experienced a sort of death. When you became a parent, so much of the life you knew passed away. Think about it. It has to be a fact that every parent has uttered this exact question: What did I do with all my free time before I had this child!?! Your free time, your sleep patterns, your spending habits, your travel plans, your friendships, your marriage—everything changed forevermore once you became a parent. No matter what happens from now on, you will never *not* be a parent. You will never be the same as you were before kids. And sometimes that can feel like a death.

And it can also feel like a rebirth. Just as a baby is born and delivered into our care, so we begin a new, radical growth process of our own. Both child and parent are in this growth process together; both are facing new challenges as they relate to one another.

For parents, the difference is that we are responsible for setting the parameters of the relationship. In other words, it's up to us to shape the rules of how to handle the inherent anxiety involved in such a close relationship. How we handle our growing pains will directly influence how the rest of the family handles their own growing pains.

In his remarkable books,[1] Dr. David Schnarch urges us to think of all relationships as people-growing machines. Relationships are supposed to be difficult because they are designed to challenge us toward personal growth. I believe this is especially true when it comes to parenting. Nothing else demands that we grow in patience and support skills as much as being a parent. No other situation requires as much consistency and integrity. Nowhere else do we feel quite as vulnerable and unqualified as when we are faced with the task of helping a needy and dependent child become a self-directed adult.

Part of being a grown-up, though, is the willingness to endure discomfort now for the sake of a payoff later. What's the payoff? Maturity, both for our children and for ourselves. And, as you'll see throughout this book, seeking our own maturity makes for a vibrant, stimulating, and mutually loving relationship with each of our children.

**Part of being a grown-up is enduring discomfort
now for the sake of a payoff later.**

But such a relationship depends on whether we choose to accept the difficulty of parenting as a challenge, an opportunity for our own growth. When we choose to grow, we can actually appreciate the fact that pain and anxiety can assist us to grow further. This attitude increases the chances that we will approach parenting with a renewed focus on ourselves, not our children, as the number-one agents for our own peace and contentment. The difficult times with our kids become necessary for our continued development; now those difficult times have meaning. Viewed in this light, our struggles are infused with purpose. And as our perspective changes, we won't be nearly as tempted to resent these children when they just won't cooperate.

The Challenge of Reactivity

A coaching client of mine once witnessed a woman and her daughter at a local coffee shop. While waiting in line, the little girl kept hanging on a swinging employees' gate.

After repeated pleading (and numerous threats), the mother finally blurted out, "IF YOU DON'T LET GO OF THAT DOOR, I'M GOING TO EMBARRASS YOU IN FRONT OF ALL THESE PEOPLE!"

Ah, the irony. Like the nice-hat episode I painfully recounted earlier, this story illustrates who really has something to be embarrassed about. That's the price of this kind of reactivity. And it's an epidemic. Just look around. How often do you see people get irrationally defensive? How often do you see parents give up, cave in, and check out?

Does this sound familiar? You've had one of those days at work, you somehow managed to get toner dust all over your new pants, and then you get a call from your daughter on her cell phone.

"Hey, Mom, where are you? You were supposed to be here half an hour ago."

Oops—today is your day to pick up the kids at school. You just want to get home and change clothes, but now you've got to rush over to the school. And you've got to get to the grocery store or it's pizza for the third night this week. You crank up the van and the tank is on empty. You get the kids and go to the store (without the shopping list because you left it at the office) and the kids start the dreaded "Ws"—the Whining Wants. Once that starts, you start the "STOP ITs" and the "I SAID NOs."

Their Ws might subside for a bit as you bark at these darling angels, but the kids are every bit as stressed as you are—and they didn't choose to come to the store. When you finally get to the checkout line, your youngest can only see the shiny, sweet things placed exactly at her eye level (brilliant marketing move or diabolical plot?), and the Whining Wants return. And, of course, the lady in front of you is paying with an out-of-state, two-party check and has a stack of coupons.

It seems your only choice is either to give in or to flip out. Of course, if you give in to one kid, then the others go for the kill, even the older ones. And if you even think about saying no to one after you've said yes to another, be prepared for the fairness fight. Children discover the concept of equity early in life. More often than not, for most of us, the flip-out is inevitable, even after the give-in.

"STOP IT RIGHT NOW!"

"WHY CAN'T YOU TWO JUST BE QUIET? WE'LL BE HOME IN A MINUTE!"

"IF YOU DON'T LET GO OF THAT RIGHT NOW, I'M GOING TO EMBARRASS YOU IN FRONT OF ALL THESE PEOPLE!"

Sometimes these lovely terms of endearment are accompanied by the arm-yank, the ear-tug, or the dreaded finger-wag. If the situation gets really heated, a head-slap or a neck-grab may even make an appearance.

Before Paul Reiser starred in the TV show *Mad About You*, he had one of the leading roles in a less popular show called *My Two Dads*, where he played the father of a teenage girl. Whenever I see a parent resort to the finger-wagging style of screaming, I remember the time Reiser's character was doing the same: lecturing his daughter while performing a serious finger-wag.

But in the middle of the lecture he stopped himself, looked at his hand, and posed this question: "When did I grow my father's finger?"

All he needed was a silly paper hat.

We all know the definition of insanity, right? Doing the same thing over and over again, expecting a different result. Can you recall a time when you panicked and flipped out and it actually helped?

Usually our reactivity causes the very outcome we most fear. And that's the price of reactivity. Consider it a rule of the universe: Whenever we give in to our anxious reactivity, we help create the very outcome we're hoping to avoid. Reactivity doesn't just make things worse; it actually helps produce the very results we're reacting against.

Whenever we give in to our anxiety, we create the very outcome we're hoping to avoid.

Something that happened to me a few years ago provides a remarkable illustration of this rule. Thankfully, it also provides a remarkable illustration of the power of a nonreactive presence, which is what ScreamFree Parenting is all about.

An Opportunity for Growth

We bought our first house when our daughter, Hannah, was four years old. Our son, Brandon, had just turned two. The kids were fascinated with all of the newness—their rooms, the new playground in the backyard, and, most of all, the steep staircase in the two-story foyer. The staircase was attached to one wall, leaving a long banister on the unattached side and nothing but hardwood floors below.

It took all of one day for Hannah to discover the thrill of climbing up the stairs on the outside of the banister. With just enough overhang to stand on, and plenty of support pickets to hang on to, this banister provided an indoor climbing adventure. Thankfully, I noticed the expedition before she got in over her head (or literally climbed above mine). I told her to come down and instructed her that climbing the outside of the stairs was off-limits.

What I didn't notice, however, was Brandon watching his big sister's every move.

Two weeks later, I walked out of my bedroom at the top of the stairs to find my smiling, adorable two-year-old halfway up the stairs, balancing on the few inches of overhang on the outside of the banister.

"Hi, Daddy."

I'm surprised I even heard him. All I could focus on at the moment were the six feet that separated him from the hardwood floors below.

What would you have done at that moment? Try to honestly gauge your level of anxiety just reading this story. In the comfort of your cozy couch, try to picture your child's beaming face perched precariously close to total disaster. What do you feel? Where do you feel it? In your gut? Between your shoulder blades? Call it anxiety, call it dread, call it nerves.

Whatever you call it, know this: That feeling is real, it is common, and it's actually here to help us. That's right. It's here to help us. No other feeling we experience is able to tell us more about ourselves than this anxiety. Thus, no other feeling is able to call us to personal growth like this anxiety.

Life's relationships seem to be designed this way, inherently producing this feeling. If you think about it, our anxiety actually occurs more often and more intensely as we get closer to someone. Rather than provide us the comfort we think we need, close relationships increase the probability that we will experience profound pain. Our closest relationships, particularly those under one roof, actually increase the level of anxiety in our lives. Bummer, huh?

Not really. It's not a bummer if we're able to reach a point in our growth where we can choose to experience this anxiety as helpful and even necessary. Rather than allowing our anxiety to provoke us to correct others, what if we took those feelings and looked within ourselves to their source? What does this heightened anxiety tell us about ourselves?

It doesn't necessarily mean you're a worrywart, a nervous wreck, or in need of heavy medication. Your anxiety about a loved one speaks of a live, growing passion, a deep concern and care for that person. You would have reason to be concerned if you *didn't* feel anxious watching a loved one making a potentially dangerous decision. Your anxiety, particularly when it comes to your kids, is a testament to how much you care, how much you want great things for them, how much passion you have for life itself.

Whenever you experience this kind of anxiety, it's a call for your own growth. Congratulations! You have entered a customized opportunity designed specifically for your personal growth. You may not have asked for it, and you can always choose *not* to grow through it. Growth is always optional—your choice. You can choose to simply give in to your anxiety instead, but as we discussed earlier, you will pay a price. Remember, emotional reactivity has the uncanny ability to help create the very outcome you're hoping to prevent.

Growth is always optional—your choice.

Which reminds me—there's a little boy left dangling from the ledge of the stairs! With my anxiety shooting through the roof, this situation was obviously my own personal growth opportunity. So let's take a moment to evaluate my options (and we always have options).

I could have chosen, of course, to do nothing and go on about my business. Giving in to anxiety ("screaming") can take several forms, including running away. Who knows what would have happened if I'd done that. The worst possible scenario would have been that he reached the top and tried to climb over the banister, only to fall backward all the way to the floor. What's the growth potential for me in this scenario? Not much—I would have chosen to avoid it.

My next option was giving in to my anxiety and getting reactive—screaming or lunging or flinching. This would have been understandable, right? My son was in mortal danger and I needed to save him. But think through what might have happened if I'd allowed myself to react in that way. I actually could have frightened him into falling.

This is the dilemma that faces us every time we interact with our kids. Our children don't have to be in mortal danger in order for us to find ourselves in a growth opportunity. Every interaction with our children, every tiny conversation and every huge argument, carries the potential for everyone's growth. We'll address those interactions throughout this book. But back to the stairs.

So what did I do? I had begun presenting the Scream-Free Parenting material publicly by this time, so I felt an extra motivation to remain calm. "Okay, Mr. ScreamFree, what the heck do you do now?" I asked myself. Nothing like having your professional reputation tied to your parenting skills.

So what did I do? I grew up a little. This was not a situation I could escape with any sense of integrity; it was a sit-uation I could embrace for my own growth and my son's benefit. My son needed me to be two things at the same time: calm *and* connected.

I did what I didn't think I could. I created a *pause*. I knew that the key to growing up was to first calm down, and I knew that I could not do so while staring at my son staring danger in the face. So I actually closed my eyes. After a pause, I reopened my eyes and acknowledged him without paying too much attention, saying "Hey, buddy," and then gently and slowly I moved down the stairs, keeping one eye in front of me and one eye back on him. He kept climbing. After what seemed like an eternity, I reached the bottom of the stairs, walked up behind him, stretched up to reach his legs, and gently, but firmly, brought him down to safety, holding him tightly in a loving embrace. Then I screamed at him to never do that to me again! (Just kidding.)

A potential disaster had been avoided. I had somehow discovered a resource within me, a place of calm resolve. I grew. I entered the opportunity, stayed in the opportunity, and grew through the experience.

The Benefits of Growth

Now let's talk about you. If you're reading this book, you're probably a frustrated parent. You might be facing so many potential "opportunities" for growth that you just want to run away. Congratulations! Life hasn't given up on you yet. The very fact that you face challenging, even overwhelming situations is a testimony to this. For some reason, the universe seems interested in your personal growth.

But we're the grown-ups, aren't we? By this time in our lives, shouldn't we be finished growing? Not by a long shot. It's more important now than ever to continue our own growth process, inviting our kids to watch us struggle to learn and grow.

What you want is for your kids to talk with you, share their lives with you. When you overreact to the information they disclose, you send mixed signals. If you want your kids to eliminate you as a resource for guidance and support, then by all means stop growing. Continue to escalate in your reactions and allow your anxiety to guide your responses.

However, if you want to be the calm influence, the "cool" parent your children really need, then do everyone a favor: Keep growing up.

As you learned earlier, it's not about them, it's about you.

Reflection Questions

1. What's the part of parenting that you find the most challenging? Think about the challenges throughout your parenting history and those you find most difficult right now.

2. Several people have said this: "I was a much better parent before I had kids." How is your view of parenting different now than it was before you had children? How is parenting more challenging? How is it more rewarding?

3. Recall an incident where your reactivity actually made things worse. What could you have done differently? What's a possible different outcome?

4. How much do you consider yourself a grown-up? How has becoming a parent asked you to continue growing?

5. What benefit might it have for your child to see you still striving toward maturity, still seeking your own growth?

Storytime

This first story illustrates the amazing power of taking the focus off your kids and placing it squarely on yourself.

Julianne knew she had to change something. After another screaming match with her thirteen-year-old daughter, Annie, she realized this was not simply a series of isolated fights; this was the dominant form of all her interactions with her daughter. As a single parent, she felt stretched so thin all the time that her emotional resources seemed depleted.

This was going nowhere.

However, instead of seeking help from outside the family, Julianne constantly, albeit unknowingly, asked her children for the kind of emotional and behavioral support they simply weren't equipped to provide. This meant needing them to perform well in school, for instance, giving their mother one less thing to worry about. Or never arguing with her, especially when she'd had a bad day. Because she was not focusing on herself, Julianne was trapped in the relational dynamic of needing her children to comply or perform for her sake, and it was not working. Her relationships with her kids were not only worn out, they were deteriorating.

It was at that point Julianne began focusing on herself, learning to recognize her part of the continuing patterns, especially with Annie. In order to grow as a mother and as a person, Julianne began to realize she needed support from other adults outside her immediate family. She started to lean on a pastor at her church. He told her she could call the next time she felt scared that she would say something that she would regret. Julianne was learning to focus less on her daughter, recognizing that the more she focused on herself instead, the more she found herself able to be calm and connected at the same time.

But as relationships change, the natural anxiety increases. As Julianne was shifting her focus and improving her ability to remain calm, Annie kept testing Mom's newfound growth.

At one point, Annie wanted to go away for the weekend with some girlfriends. One of the other girls' parents was going to pay for the trip, and they were to stay at a hotel, just for fun. Julianne's radar went off when she realized the girls were going to be "dropped off" for the weekend, with no adult supervision. She told Annie an emphatic no. This set off an intense scene, to say the least.

Annie erupted with more intensity than ever before, and Julianne's newfound calm was put to the test. In the midst of Annie's horrendous screaming fit ("You never let me do anything!" "You're so unfair!" "I hate you!"), Julianne turned her back on her daughter and went into her own bedroom. (Sometimes we need a break in order to remain calm.) She closed the door behind her, shutting Annie out. In tears, this exasperated mom immediately went to the phone and called her pastor. It was eleven in the evening, but she was at her wits' end. The pastor didn't mind at all. But her daughter did.

Annie barged in, screaming "Oh, who're you calling? Someone to listen to you complain about me? That's just great!" Then she stormed out of the room.

But Julianne did not acquiesce to her daughter's reaction. Instead, she began talking to her pastor about herself. She did not complain even once about Annie.

"I'm angry," she said on the phone, "and I'm tempted to say things I don't mean."

She told him she was tired and not very good at taking care of herself, especially with all the demands of single parenthood.

"I'm angry at myself most of all."

Julianne was doing a great job of maintaining her focus on herself. They talked for several minutes, and with each sentence she became calmer. Simply talking about her own emotions was helping her take the focus off her daughter. Choosing to examine herself was taking the fire out of her belly and allowing her deepest desires for her relationship with her daughter to come to the surface.

As Julianne's peace began to defeat her anxiety, she noticed Annie's face peering from around the door. Apparently, after she had stormed out of the room, Annie had come back and put her ear to the door; she had been listening the entire time. When Julianne noticed and looked back, Annie quickly pulled the door shut to conceal her eavesdropping.

After the phone conversation was over and Julianne felt confidently calm, she left her room and headed down the hall to her daughter's. When she got there, the lights were out and Annie was in bed. Julianne decided to leave well enough alone until the next day.

That morning was a completely different scene. Her daughter did not come down and graciously apologize, but she did calmly say that she understood her mother's point of view. She had obviously focused on herself that night as well, because she was then able to articulate what was really bothering her.

"I understand you're just trying to do what's best for me, Mom. I really do. I just feel like you never want me to grow up."

Julianne was able to listen with calm and connection. She was able to hear her daughter's views and express her own concerns about the weekend excursion. The conversation ended with a hug and tears. Evidently, Annie's eavesdropping ears heard quite a bit the night before. She heard that her mom wasn't trying to control her; she was trying to control herself. Julianne's short dialogue with her pastor spoke volumes to Annie.

She didn't need a heated speech from her mom, she needed a mom committed to focusing on herself, growing herself up, and calming herself down. And that's what Julianne was beginning to give her.

Annie didn't go away that weekend. At her own request, she went shopping with Mom instead.

PART TWO

Keeping Your Cool
Means Creating *Space*

When they were very small I suppose I thought
someday they would become who they were because of
what I'd done. Now I suspect they simply grew into
their true selves because they demanded in a thousand
ways that I back off and let them be.

—ANNA QUINDLEN, "GOODBYE, DR. SPOCK," *Newsweek*

You've come a long way so far. In the first part of this
book, you learned that in order to have the best relationships with your kids, you need to focus on yourself, calm yourself down, and grow yourself up. Now we
shift a bit.

As you become a calming authority in your home, your
influence begins to shift. Instead of shaping your family system with your anxiety, creating the kind of relationships

you're hoping to avoid, you begin to influence through the *absence* of your anxiety. Your calm presence empowers you to become more available as an inspiration to your children, which engenders profound levels of trust and respect.

What do you do with this growing calm and this new-found level of authority? You continue with what brought you here—you focus on yourself and your responsibility *to* your children. In the next two parts, we're going to look at creating and maintaining an environment that facilitates your children's growth. And, as you know by now, the greatest factor in your children's growth process is your *own* continued growth as a parent. So it makes sense to shape your environment in a way that helps you remain both calm and connected.

And that means it's time to talk about boundaries.

Recently many authors and relationship experts have been banging the drum for a better understanding of *boundaries*. In fact, the concept has become commonplace; the word itself as applied to human relationships has entered our vernacular. But when a relationship concept becomes popular, it is easy to get confused about what it really means.

I'm not going to say that the concept of boundaries is simple, but I will try to give as simple a definition as possible. Here goes: Your boundaries refer to your *space* and your *place*. Space and place—easy to remember, right? Your *space* is the emotional and physical territory you occupy in the world. Your *place* is the fence around your space, the limits of your freedom as it bumps up against other people's space.

And that's it: Boundaries are about your space and your place.

The section you are about to read focuses on creating space. We all need our space—space to breathe our own air, space to grow, and space to discover ourselves. In this space, we get to know our preferences, our temptations, and our tendencies. In this space, we learn about our strengths and weaknesses, and we learn about our needs and our wants. In short, it is within our space that we develop our sense of self, our sense of individuality.

As parents, it is our responsibility to our children to create and maintain a family environment that encourages and honors this space, for each person in the family.

The next four chapters will show you that choosing to keep your cool, choosing to be ScreamFree, is the best way to create and maintain this healthy space.

And more important, creating space is the best way to help you to remain ScreamFree.

CHAPTER FOUR

Begin with the End in Mind, but Let Go of the Final Results

After seeing my newborn baby for the first time, I now know for a fact that I'm on my way out. Let us make no mistake about why these babies are here: they are here to replace us.

—Jerry Seinfeld

Life does not begin at the moment of conception or the moment of birth. It begins when the kids leave home and the dog dies.

—Unknown

Years before *Bringing Down the House*, Steve Martin played his first struggling father character in the movie *Parenthood*. In the film, Martin does a remarkable job showing the roller coaster of emotions we tie to our children's behaviors. He also shows the pitfalls of taking too much responsibility for how they turn out.

After he has an especially effective moment with his struggling son, he begins to daydream about his son's college graduation ceremony. As the son delivers his valedictorian speech, he thanks "the most important and influential person" in his life, his father. An elderly Steve Martin stands up to the crowd's applause and his son goes on to recall a moment in his childhood when he was having a rough time.

"But thanks to my dad," he recalls, "I am now the most outstanding, the most confident, and the most well-adjusted person in this world."

A little later in the movie, Steve Martin's son has a major meltdown, and again Dad fantasizes about his overestimated responsibility. In this daydream/nightmare, the scene is chaos on a college campus. In a re-creation of Charles Whitman's 1966 University of Texas massacre, we see Martin's son perched on top of the tallest building on campus, shooting his rifle at random victims. The police give a megaphone to Martin, hoping the father can talk the son down. Instead, Steve Martin is completely befuddled, trying to coax his son with pop-psych self-esteem techniques.

"Good shot, son!" he yells after another successful kill. With a shrug, he explains to bystanders, "It's important to be supportive."

The Paradox of Parenting

We all have fantasies about how our children will turn out. We think about their college choices and career possibilities, and we wonder when they might start a family of their own. Some of us even think about our own lives then, traveling to visit our grown children and spoiling our own precious grandkids. These fantasies are precious and usually occur during those wonderful moments when we feel great about our relationships with each child.

At other moments, however, our fantasies also become nightmares. We fear all the potential traps out there and we dread that our child may not have what it takes to make it out in the world. Usually these fear-filled moments occur when our relationship with our child is *not* going well, when all we feel is the frustration of seeing her make the same mistake yet again.

Like Steve Martin's character in *Parenthood*, we have each vacillated between fantasies of success and failure, depending on how we're feeling at the moment. And, like Martin, we're not exactly sure how to estimate our influence, or gauge our responsibility, in those outcomes.

What we know we face is a paradox. On one hand, we know parents are the most powerful influence in the lives of children and, thus, parents play the most important role on the planet in terms of shaping the future of humanity. On the other hand, we know parents cannot be held totally responsible for the choices of their children; to do so would negate the very responsibility of parents to train their children for responsible adulthood. And children cannot ever hold their parents responsible for their own choices without sacrificing the very individuality they crave.

So we have a paradox. Parents shape their children. Children shape themselves. Both are true. My answer to this paradox is not to eliminate it but rather embrace it by changing one small preposition: We are not responsible *for* our children; we are responsible *to* them.

We examined this earlier in the first chapter. As we begin this new section, looking at the type of environment you want to create in your home, we need to revisit the issue. As you learned earlier, having a responsibility *for* your kids necessarily orbits your life around your kids, needing them to perform so you know you've done a good job as a parent. It also necessitates a technique-driven approach to your parenting, employing whatever behavioral program you can to ensure they turn out as well as you need them to. This does not make for ScreamFree Parenting. This makes for anxiety-driven, relationship-damaging parenting.

So we have a paradox. Parents shape their children. Children shape themselves. Both are true.

But all of this does not mean you turn a blind eye or deaf ear to the outcomes you'd like to help bring about for your kids. I would never advocate a passive, sit-back-and-hope-for-the-best style of parenting. No, you are responsible to your children for whatever you do to help them make it in the world. So, it's vitally important to take a more intentional look at the type of results you're looking to accomplish. And this means you need to take a serious look at the lasting relationships you would like to have with each of your children.

Beginning with the End in Mind

I've borrowed the title of this chapter from Stephen Covey. "Begin with the End in Mind" is the second chapter of *The Seven Habits of Highly Effective People*, Covey's landmark book on human potential. In that chapter, Covey leads the reader through an imaging exercise. He asks us to picture our funeral, down to the last detail, especially the attendees. We are to specifically imagine whom we would like to eulogize us and what they would have to say. By imaging what we would love others to say about us then, we can see our deepest priorities and principles now. Thus we can organize our present life around those principles, bringing into effect the results we have already imagined in our minds.

That's how the exercise works. And it can be tremendously helpful. What we're going to do here in this chapter is very similar. I'm going to lead you in an exercise to visualize the type of adult you want each of your children to become and the type of relationship you would like to enjoy with each of them. Most important, you will begin to see the type of growth you would like for yourself.

Begin by relocating yourself to a quiet place, isolated from the noise and clutter of kids, spouses, housework, and television. Now begin to visualize your youngest child at the age of twenty-five. What year is it? How old does that make each of your other children? How old does that make you? After you've done all the math, allow yourself to get really imaginative. I want you to think about each of your children and ponder your ideal for the following questions.

Allow yourself to truly long for this ideal, how you would love it to be, in each of these areas.

- Are your children married? For how long?
- How would you rate their marriages?
- Do they have children? How would you rate your children as parents?
- Do they have college degrees? Master's degrees? What was their major? What do they do for work?
- How much money do they make? Do they work for a large corporation, or do they have an entrepreneurial vision?

These might be the most important questions:

- What is the content of their character?
- What do their friends and spouses say about them? Their bosses and coworkers?
- How self-sufficient are they? What is their decision-making process?
- How well do they take responsibility for their choices?
- Are they physically healthy and active? How well do they take care of their bodies?
- What are your grown children's deepest values? How do they contribute to society?
- How do they carry themselves around others?
- How do they spend their alone time?
- What are their spiritual beliefs, and how do those beliefs shape their worldview?

Now the tough part. Recall again how old you'll be at that time. Start to imagine your future.

- Are you married? How do you rate your marriage?
- How healthy are you physically? How well do you take care of your body?
- Where do you live? Are you still working, or have you retired? How do you spend your days?
- How have you grown and matured?

Now focus on your relationship with your kids.

- How often do you see your grown children? What type of relationship do you have with them? Are you close? Distant? At each other's throats? Too close for comfort?
- How much respect do you and your children have for each other as individuals? Are you still waiting for one of your children to grow up?
- Do you still support them financially? Do any of them still live under your roof? Do you live under one of theirs?
- How would you rate yourself as a grandparent?
- Are your grown children inspired by you, your success and your maturity? How do they talk about you to their spouses, their friends, their children?

Congratulations. To whatever extent you were able to put some serious thought to those questions, you have every reason to be proud of yourself. Why? Because while we may occasionally fantasize about the future, hardly any of us allow ourselves to truly think ahead like that. We are so quick to put off such future imagining as nothing more than irresponsible, wishful thinking. And yet these ideas often reflect the deepest desire of our hearts.

I love C. S. Lewis's thought on the matter. When criticized for urging readers to concentrate on their deepest longings for the future, Lewis came back with a quick but profound retort. He said not to think of it as wishful thinking but rather "thoughtful wishing."

What goals do you have for your parenting?

And that's what you've just done. What's amazing about the process is that the more we engage in thoughtful wishing, the more we find ourselves drawn to actions today that have the best chance of producing those results tomorrow.

That's what it means to begin with the end in mind. By intentionally focusing on the outcome we desire for tomorrow, we encourage ourselves to take the most effective actions today. So, to what end are you working? What goals do you have for this entire parenting journey?

By taking you through this journey, I led you to reflect on a future when your child is an adult. And that is the entire goal of parenting—to produce another adult.

As Jerry Seinfeld said, it is our child's job to eventually replace us. And that's the paradox. It is our job to both train our children for that job and get out of the way as they learn to do it. Like the old saying, we can lead a horse to water, but we cannot make it drink. That's why we have to practice . . .

Letting Go of the Final Results

So much of the business world is based on getting desired results. Managers are fired because they did not produce the desired results on the bottom line. Sales brochures and commercials do nothing but promote guaranteed results. We want to know if we apply this product in the correct manner, we will definitely see the promised results. That's why so many parenting books promise what we want to hear: Apply this program and you will definitely see more obedient, cooperative, and loving children. We guarantee this technique will result in the behavioral changes you so desire. "What works for Fido will work for your child!"

Fortunately, life doesn't work that way.

Children are not machines or pets, and parents are neither their operators nor their owners. When it comes to relationships, we cannot ever guarantee or control the end we desire. While working toward that end, we must let go of the need to achieve it. That's the paradox we mentioned earlier. And it is aggravating.

"You mean even though I want my child to turn out to be a loving, responsible adult, I can't focus on turning my child into a loving, responsible adult?"

Exactly. Here's why. The more you focus on producing the result for your child that you desire, the less chance your child has of authentically choosing that result for herself. The more it becomes *your* goal, the less room she has to discover *her own* goal.

I speak a lot at churches and to religious groups. One of the primary concerns of any faith community is training their children to love and honor God. For most people of faith, that is the number-one goal of parenting. Thus, they are a little put off when I assert that this is actually not their most important goal. Again and again I tell them that launching their children into a self-directed adulthood is far more important.

Why? Because if your child is not a self-directed adult, then whatever faith he does develop will not truly be his own. He cannot authentically choose to follow God if he cannot choose, on his own, to follow God. Such a faith would be a borrowed faith at best, one that is still seeking to appease or please others. Again, this brings up the paradox for parents. If you want to make sure your child follows God, then you have to let go of your need to make sure your child follows God. You need to create a space for your child to develop a relationship with God on his own terms. Does that mean you do nothing? Of course not. You actively create faith discussions throughout your child's development. You introduce him to the faith tradition that's led you thus far, and, above all, you live in a way that reflects the highest values of that faith. But you cannot force your child to follow that way, because then he would not develop an authentic faith of his own.

Again, begin with the end in mind. Lead the horse to water . . . We are training children ultimately to become responsible for themselves and no one else. The ultimate goal of parenting is to launch our children into an adulthood where they are self-directed, decisive, and responsible people.

Think about it. What is the number-one complaint of parents, particularly those with teenagers? Their children do not take responsibility for their own actions. It is no co-incidence, therefore, that the number-one hope of parents is that their children become adults who are able to do just that, take responsibility for their actions. This means they are *self-directed*. That may not be a term you're familiar with, so here are the attributes of a self-directed adult:

- He knows and pursues what he wants in life.
- She gladly seeks counsel from others, but ultimately makes up her own mind.
- He demonstrates integrity, a consistency of his beliefs, desires, words, and actions.
- She holds people accountable for their actions (including her parents), but does not blame others for her own problems.
- He does not let others blame him for their problems.
- She gladly and quickly takes responsibility for her decisions.
- He welcomes criticism as feedback, but does not automatically accept it as truth.
- She takes care of herself in order to be available to others without needing them to take care of her.

Aren't these the very attributes you hope for your children? Aren't these the qualities you want them to demonstrate, the qualities that give them the best chance of success in this world? What environment do you need to create in your home that can best lead them to develop those qualities? Here's the crux: If you want your children to become self-directed adults, you have to face the truth that you cannot do it for them. In truth, the more you try to make them into self-directed adults, the less chance they have of becoming such adults.

If you want your children to become self-directed adults, you have to face the truth that you cannot do it for them.

Launching Our Kids into Adulthood

What's the answer? Continuing to focus on ourselves. If we want to produce self-directed adults, first we each have to become one ourselves. Especially in relationship to our children. This means creating space for them to make decisions and calming our anxiety about those decisions. This means teaching them the principles of life and then letting them decide whether to accept them and follow them or to fight against them and suffer the consequences.

Back when I taught high school seniors, I had the opportunity to witness parents who were able to let go of the final results and parents who were not. For those who were unable, that senior year was a nightmare. As the idea of leaving for college became closer to reality, the anxiety level of the whole family system shot right through the roof.

In response to that increasing anxiety, these parents gave in to it, beginning to micromanage every aspect of their child's life. They would hover over every homework assignment, tighten the leash on social activities, and constantly check up on the college application process. And it saddened me to watch as their relationships with their children deteriorated.

Other parents would respond to this stress differently. They looked on this senior year as one step closer to liftoff and thus used it as a chance to hand more and more direction over to their child. This wasn't easy, to be sure, and these parents struggled as they watched their child make decisions. But these parents stuck to their principle of calming their own anxiety instead of asking their child to calm it for them. During the college application process, they would hand over the forms to their son and let him know they were there to provide help if he needed any. These parents would actually extend their daughter's curfew a little later for that senior year, giving both themselves and their child a taste of what it would be like the following year, when dorm life most likely wouldn't come with a curfew at all.

In truth, these senior year experiences for all these families were not unexpected, given the parent-child relationships up to that point. For those parents who had always dreaded thinking about the future launching, who had always needed their child to perform for their sake, and who chose *not* to pursue their child's self-direction, that senior year was a logical extension of what had come before. They encountered the enormous battle of trying to rein their child in while the child strained desperately to get more and more "freedom." By the time senior year came around, neither parent nor child was anywhere near ready for the launching process to begin and each would just blame the other for all the problems it created. Thankfully, a number of those families sought professional help, from me and others, and parent and child alike were able to develop the courage to look at themselves and choose to calm down and grow up.

For those parents who had always been training their child for self-direction, however, that senior year went much more smoothly. These were the parents who had progressively extended the freedom and responsibility of their growing children, knowing that was the best way to train them for liftoff. It was still an anxious time, for sure. But it was an excited anxiety, full of planning and dreaming. It was also an experience of trial and error, as both parents and children struggled through the ramifications of increased self-direction. But regardless of the mistakes made, these parents had committed to the principle of beginning with the end in mind and letting go of the final results.

You can too.

Reflection Questions

1. What was it like for you to imagine your and your family's future? What was the hardest part? What did you like thinking about the most?

2. When you think about your effect on your child's future, what is your first feeling: excitement, hope, fear, guilt, dread?

3. If you can be honest with yourself, how much do you hope your children fulfill *your own* ambitions? How well do you know *their* ambitions?

4. How self-directed is each of your children now? What steps have they taken recently toward self-direction, and how have you encouraged that growth?

5. What does it mean to you to "let go of the final results"? What might that look like in terms of your relationships with your children?

CHAPTER FIVE

Kids Need Their Room

The children who do best are the ones
least essential to our own salvation.
—EDWIN H. FRIEDMAN, *Friedman's Fables*

What children need most are parents who do not need them. I know that sentence is a bit jarring, so read it again. Now, let's unpack that a bit. What children need most is for their parents to be the first ones who see them as individuals in their own right, with their own lives and decisions and futures. Children were not put on this earth to make us parents feel loved, warm, respected, or appreciated. They were put here to *become themselves* by becoming self-directed adults. And they need for us to create enough space to do just that.

Now, before this sounds too much like the permissive parenting of the 1960s, or some cold and aloof method of detachment, let's remember what we've said about space.

Your space is your territory. It's your freedom and your responsibility to occupy a certain territory in the universe. At its most basic, this means the physical space your body occupies. Your body occupies a space that cannot be occupied by anyone or anything else. In America, most bodies take up more than their fair share of space, but that's a topic for another book. (Look for *ScreamFree Weight Loss* sometime in the future.)

But a person's space doesn't stop with just her body.

Your space extends beyond your body to your "personal space," such as the distance you like to maintain in a crowded airport, especially from those big guys who wear tank tops in public. Just as importantly, your space also includes your emotional freedom to explore different feelings, ranging from anger, to sadness, to confusion. Space includes your inner space for self-reflection, self-definition, and self-understanding. Privacy, opinion, attitude, thought—all find their home in your space.

In defining the word "kingdom," Dallas Willard, professor of philosophy at the University of Southern California, writes:

> Every last one of us has a "kingdom"—or a "queendom," or a "government"—a realm that is uniquely our own, where our choice determines what happens. . . . Our "kingdom" is simply the range of our effective will. Whatever we genuinely have say over is in our kingdom.[1]

In other words, each of us has a space we can call our own. In that space, we have the freedom to explore, to discover possibilities and potential, to make mistakes and learn from them. In that space, we can be comfortable and learn to struggle through our discomfort. We don't have to put on a mask or pretend. We can be ourselves with no fear or shame.

Each of us has a space to call our own.

Every person ever born, including each of your children, was designed to have a space like this. It's part of why we don't like being told what to do. It's why we learn in our earliest years to say things like "You're not the boss of me!"

Most two-year-old children have a favorite word: NO! Why is it their favorite word? It's not because they're necessarily rebellious, and it's not because they're absolutely depraved little criminals. A two-year-old's favorite word is NO! because she's learning to develop her sense of her own space. In fact, the sense of having some measure of control over things is a vital factor in both mental and physical health.

I remember watching my daughter when she was two, learning to separate herself from us. On one occasion she looked straight at me, held her arms out as if to push me away, and said, "Don't follow me!"

And then she ran into her room by herself.

A few minutes later she came back out (checking to see that I was still there) and said again, "Don't come after me into my room!"

She again ran into her room for a few minutes of alone time. I could have chosen to take this personally, getting reactive to the idea that she didn't want to play with me anymore. I could have also taken this fearfully, getting reactive to the idea that she's too young be alone, that she might hurt herself. But what was really going on? My daughter was developing a sense of her own space. She wanted to play by herself to see if she could. She ran out to see me again because she wanted to know I was still there.

**Without space to make their own mistakes,
our kids live only borrowed lives.**

I've chosen the word "room" in this chapter title because it conveys both the physical and the emotional space our kids need to fully become themselves. Just listen to our language. "Room" not only refers to a physical location, as in "Don't follow me into my room." It also relates to a sense of freedom, as in "room to grow" and "breathing room." I've also chosen the word "room" because it refers to a literal battleground in most American homes—the child's messy room—which actually provides an amazing growth opportunity for both parent and child. More on that later.

Kids need their "room" because without adequate space to explore, experiment, and, yes, make their own decisions, they can never fully become the self-directed adults we want them to be. This does not mean each child needs his or her own literal room in the house. (Only a small percentage of the world's families have the financial wherewithal to allow for that.) Rather, I am talking about the principle of granting each of your children his or her own kingdom, which includes physical space—their bodies, their privacy while in the bathroom, a small corner, or a whole room—and emotional space.

Without space to learn their own likes and dislikes, without space to make their own mistakes, our kids continue to live borrowed lives, and it leaves them with only two choices: fight against everyone's efforts to determine their life (the rebellious child) or simply defer to everyone around them (the passive, robotic child).

Space Out

You've probably figured out by now that creating space means creating some separation. But families aren't supposed to be separated, right?

On more than one occasion I've received a strong objection to this part of the material. During several ScreamFree Parenting seminars, people have stood up and protested that theirs was "not a closed-doors family." They strongly argued there should not be any distance within the family, that privacy and respect for each other's space is not a high priority. Togetherness is their highest priority.

Going back to our goal of launching our children into self-direction, my question to these objecting parents is always the same: "Until when? At what point will you recognize your children's right to privacy, to their own space? When they're old enough to drive? When they leave the house? When they get married?" If we're beginning with the end in mind, then why not teach this model of respect in the single most influential environment our children will ever know? Why not model now the respect we want them to exhibit later, respect both for themselves and for others?

Don't you want your daughter to respect herself enough to ward off boys and their efforts to cajole her into premature sexual activity? Then you model how she deserves to be treated by respecting her privacy, her own space, starting tonight. Teach her that her space is respect-worthy now. Do this not merely by saying the words "You should respect yourself," but by showing her that respect first. Encourage her to close her door. Knock when you want to enter. Ask her if she wants to talk about her feelings, and respect her answer. Buy her a diary and promise that, no matter what, you will never, ever read it. And then don't even ask if she's ever used it. As she develops physically, refuse to assume you can hold and touch her as you always have. This is especially true for fathers. As the man in her life now, you should definitely continue to pursue affectionate and appropriate touch, but you should also ask permission first, and then respect her wishes. This may feel awkward, and her wishes may occasionally disappoint you, but this type of respect will shape what she expects from the men in her life later.

Since coming out of the womb, our children have been on a journey to separate from us. Even their need to bond closely at the beginning is for the express purpose of developing a sense of personal security without us later. As we learned in the last chapter, children need to separate from us to become what we all want them to be—self-directed adults. So now, when they are close to us, we can be the ones to help introduce healthy separation.

By voluntarily creating more space for our children, we remove their anxious need to separate with drugs, premature sex, gangs, or suicide. Kids do not need more of our anxious reactivity about these choices—they need more emotional space from us to learn to respect their own individuality. Hard as it may be for us to hear, it is far better for our children to make bad choices on their own than to have them run to those choices as an escape from our anxiety.

And, believe it or not, our nonanxious creation of space actually makes those bad choices far less likely. Calming ourselves down communicates so much so powerfully to our children, namely that (1) their separation from us is more than okay, it is good; and (2) our respect for them is growing, not lessening, as they get older and their choices take on more significance. This communication doesn't guarantee they won't make mistakes; nothing can do that. But calming down our anxiety about their bad choices at least removes the attraction of their doing something bad just to escape from their anxious parents.

We Cannot Call It Theirs and Still Act Like It Belongs to Us

As hard as this newfound appreciation for space might be to put into practice, we must recognize that a mutually respectful parent-child relationship must always begin with the parent. We cannot wait for our kids to respect us (and themselves) before we extend that respect to them. And in regard to space, that means we cannot determine how our children use their space any more than our kids can determine how we use ours. It is their space. It's not a privilege; it's a right. It's part of being human. Every man, woman, and child has a kingdom.

This means you cannot tell anyone else, particularly your children, how to feel. Parenting experts Scott Turansky and Joanne Miller tell a story about a mother whose four-year-old daughter sometimes gets into grumpy moods. This mother decided to take on her daughter's emotions as a challenge. She held her daughter, tickled her daughter, or made cookies with her daughter. Sometimes this "worked," but other times her daughter would just continue being grumpy.

Eventually, the mother told her daughter, "It looks like you want to be sad for a while, so there's probably not much I can do about it. Let me know when you're feeling better."

Turansky and Miller conclude the story by saying, "This mom recognized that she could do a number of things to help, but ultimately the decision to change was up to her daughter."[2]

But we don't just want to make sure they feel good. Often we want to know that our children feel regret or remorse after they've misbehaved. We think we need to change our children's hearts before we can release them out into the world. It makes us feel better if we know they at least *feel* the right way.

But it's not your job to change the hearts of your children by telling them how to think or feel. By trying to do something you aren't meant to do, you invade their space and violate their rights as people. And since this effort is led by your anxiety, you inevitably end up creating the very type of rebellious heart you were hoping to change in the first place.

The beautiful irony is that learning to respect their feelings (and their right to feel them) actually increases the chances that they will feel the way you hope they do.

In the same way that you respect this emotional space, you cannot give them a room (or any physical space in the home, even a small corner), call it theirs, and then continue to act as if it belongs to you. If it is "their" room, then it is up to them to keep, explore, clean (or not clean), and organize. That means no barging in. Knock. And ask if you may come in. Wait for them to invite you in. I know it seems weird; their room is in your house, after all. But this is what it means to extend respect for another person's space. You'd like them to give you the same respect, right? But you cannot expect that respect when you don't initiate and model it for your child.

The Power of Keeping Your Cool

This is a difficult principle because it demands you confront your own anxiety. Give my kid space? What if she starts to hide stuff from me? What if she starts to make some bad decisions? What if she hurts herself? What if she feels abandoned? What if she has to struggle? What if, what if, what if?

What is always behind our invasion of their space is, of course, our own anxious reactivity. We cannot let them struggle for too long because we need them to do it, whatever it is, quickly. We cannot let them feel bad or have a really grumpy day because that reflects on their life, which we view as our responsibility. If my kids are not happy then it must be because of something I have done, or failed to do. We get reactive about their messy room because we think they are becoming slobs, and we cannot let that happen because that would go against everything our parents taught us, and on and on and on.

What is always behind our invasion of their space is, of course, our own anxious reactivity.

We are so afraid of giving our kids their room because we fear what they might do with it. We might "give them enough rope to hang themselves." I understand this fear and I share it with you. And yes, there are certainly age-appropriate degrees of separation and space.

But becoming a ScreamFree Parent is about learning to operate out of respect for your highest principles, not in reaction to your deepest fears. You can never operate out of your fear because you will, as we learned in Part One, inevitably create the very outcome you fear. Think about the implications of continually going through your teenage son's room, looking for contraband. What does that teach your son? To become a better hider. It doesn't teach him that Dad is actually the best person to go to whenever the temptations of life kick in, that's for sure.

The importance of giving your children increasing space as they age is far greater than the fear of what they might do with that space. It has to be or you will constantly feel forced to shift your focus back on your kids, feel responsible for them, reenter the orbit around them, and so on.

The power of creating room for your kids is that you become amazed by what they do with it.

The remarkable power of creating room for your children is that you get to be amazed by what they do with it! As you reduce your anxiety about their choices, their choices begin to astound you. I know you might doubt that, because you can so accurately predict your child's responses. But I want you to listen in on this recent exchange between a coaching client and her eight-year-old daughter.

Mom was starting to respect her daughter's "room" and her daughter didn't know what to do.

DAUGHTER: Mommy, I know I have to clean my room tonight, but I'm just too tired!

MOTHER: Why do you have to clean your room, honey?

DAUGHTER: Because you guys always make me!

MOTHER: Honey, you don't have to clean your room if you don't want to. It's your room.

DAUGHTER: What? Since when?

MOTHER: Since I decided that it is your room.

DAUGHTER: But it's going to take a long time to clean it!

MOTHER: Honey, you don't have to clean it.

DAUGHTER: I don't?

MOTHER: No, not if you don't want to. But let me ask you something. Do you want it clean?

DAUGHTER: Well, I like to know where everything is.

MOTHER: Then clean it. I'll even help if you want me to.

DAUGHTER: But it'll take too long and I'm tired!

MOTHER: Then don't clean it.

[My client then started to walk away.]

DAUGHTER: But Mommy?!

MOTHER: Yes, honey?

DAUGHTER: I guess I could do a little tonight and then finish it tomorrow. It's not like I have to finish it tonight or anything.

MOTHER: That sounds like a great idea. Let me know if you want any help.

Two days later, her room was not spotless. But it was picked up and it was more organized than most other days. And the little girl was ridiculously proud of herself. I think Mommy had every reason to be proud of herself as well.

Contrast that with the battles most parents get into with their children. It has nothing to do with your child being a slob or you being a neat freak. The battle over the messy room has nothing to do with cleanliness! It also has nothing to do with the child's disrespect or ingratitude. The battle over the messy room is a battle over space. When we choose to call it "her" room, but then continue to act like the room belongs to us, we invade our child's space and eliminate the possibility that she can develop her own sense of respect for her own space.

But when we extend the same type of respect for our children's space that we want for our own, then watch out. You'll be amazed at what happens. The question is, can you calm yourself down enough to truly create space?

I believe you can.

Eight Ways to Create Space for Your Children

When you are ready to start calming your own anxiety and create more space for your children, here are some practical ways to do that. These are NOT techniques to get your children to behave, but rather practices for you to begin with the end in mind, yet let go of the final results.

1. **Respect their space and privacy.** Starting as soon as you can, calm your anxiety about letting them close the door, and make it a practice to always ask or knock before entering their room (or if they're in the bathroom) and wait to hear their response. If they say "no," then tell them you'll come back later.

2. **Calm your anxiety about their messy room.** If it is "their" room, then let them keep it the way they want to. Tell them that twice a year, for hygienic reasons, the entire house is going to be thoroughly cleaned, and that includes their room. In between those times, let their room be theirs. Whenever you feel anxious about their mess, go clean your own room. Of course, you can let them know what you think of their cleaning practices, and you can decline their invitation into their lair for your genuine fear of tripping over all the junk. But leave it at that.

3. **Respect their choices.** Give your child an allowance appropriate for her age and then let her spend it any

way she chooses. Even if you can only afford a single cent, it is the principle that counts. Go ahead and teach her about different options (investing, spending, and giving), but don't expect her to take care of her money any better than you do. When we give our children money, we give up the right to determine how that money is used. It isn't really theirs if we're going to tell them how to spend it. If you want your money spent in a certain way, then go ahead and spend it that way. It's yours to begin with! But once you give it away, you give it away. If we want kids to learn, value, and become decisive about money, then we have to allow it to become truly theirs.

4. **Calm your anxiety by giving up your need to know how they feel.** Most of the time, they simply do not know how they feel (the same is true for most adults). Your anxious need for them to know just makes it more difficult. Paradoxically, the less you need to know, the more they end up telling you. This doesn't mean neglect any concern about their feelings—this is about being calm and connected at the same time. So inquire about their feelings, show interest in helping them learn to express themselves. But let go of your need to make sure they feel the "right" way, which is nothing more than the way you think they should feel and is usually about your anxiety related to your own feelings.

5. **Similarly, give up your need to know "why."** Asking any child, from toddler to teenager, to account for

his motivation at the time of his mistake is a fruitless exercise. He simply does not know most of the time. And your need to know is much more about you than it is about him. But you want to know he can demonstrate some form of reasoning, right? You think this eases your fears about his chances out in the world and how that might reflect on you.

But here's the irony: if he did know and he was able to carefully explain his well-thought-out reason for hitting his little brother or skipping school, your fears wouldn't be eased, they'd be justified! If your son could intellectually recall his reasoning behind his choice to neglect his homework and then lie about it, you wouldn't be less scared, you'd be more fearful than ever!

"Before, I feared, in my most anxious moments, that he might be a delinquent. Now I know for sure!"

Either way, asking why has no fruitful end. At the very least, it puts the child on the defensive because you're asking him to give just that, a defense.

6. **Let them struggle.** Always answering your child's questions, or constantly telling your child what to do to solve a problem, is denying that child the chance to develop his own skills of discovery and innovation. "Mom, I can't do this!" has an uncanny ability to stir up our anxious need to fix the problem.

But if you rush to answer, then you deny them the space needed to figure things out for themselves.

Letting them struggle might look like this: "You can't? Man, that stinks. What have you tried so far?"

After their response, ask them, "So what are you going to do about it?" The more you can calm your anxiety while watching them struggle, the more you'll be amazed at their growth (and yours).

7. **Allow your kids to disagree with you and learn to respect their arguments.** This is incredibly difficult for anxious parents, but allowing (and even encouraging) your child to disagree with you creates a profound mutual respect in the parent-child relationship. Questions like "This is what I think, what do you think?" show a remarkable respect for your child as a separate individual.

   As you become more and more ScreamFree, you can actually learn to learn from your child, choosing not to "yes, but" your child's every point, but actually validating her thought process and her importance in the relationship.

8. **Rarely look your kids in the eye when talking with them.** I know this sounds absurd and even heretical. Eye-to-eye conversations are incredibly intimate, however, and bring about high levels of vulnerability. Thus, these types of conversations lend themselves to patterns of intimidation and defensiveness. Yes, there are times, sweet and nurturing as well as stern and serious, when it is very helpful to address eye to eye. But these times are rare. Use them sparingly.

   If your goal is to allow your child to explore her space and share that process with you, then engage in a common activity that takes your eyes off each other while keeping you connected. Go on a walk or a drive, build Lego projects, play a game, skip rocks, throw the baseball, go shopping, whatever. Not only does this common activity disarm you both from a defensive or aggressive posture, it also, most important, gives you the adequate space to remain calm yet connected.

And if you haven't guessed by now, that's the main point to giving your child space—it makes it easier for you to remain ScreamFree. Becoming ScreamFree helps you create space; and creating space helps you become ScreamFree. Beautiful, isn't it? And believe it or not, you're already on your way.

Reflection Questions

1. How much privacy do your children have a right to?

2. What's the hardest part about extending more and more space to your child?

3. Has your child ever marked anything—a book or a door—as "Private, Keep Out"? Have they ever pulled away from you when you've tried to embrace or kiss them? What has been your reaction?

4. What are your deepest fears about extending your child too much space?

5. How much freedom does your child have to hate you? Disagree with you? Express anger toward you and your decisions?

CHAPTER SIX

Resistance Is Futile;
Practice Judo Parenting

Resistance is futile.

—THE BORG, *Star Trek*

I have found the best way to give advice to your
children is to find out what they want and then advise
them to do it.

—HARRY S TRUMAN

No, I am not a *Star Trek* nerd. I actually make fun of
my friends who are, and I pray for them daily. But I
do like one of the villainous enemies from the show
called The Borg. They are a race of cyborgs, and they all belong to one collective consciousness. (My nerd friends had
to help me craft that sentence.) What that means is they all
have separate bodies but no thought processes or will of

their own. For The Borg, there is no such thing as individuality. When they capture others, they "assimilate" them into their collective being, erasing any individuality of the captured. From what you've read so far, you can see that The Borg do the exact opposite of creating space—they eliminate it. They are so powerful in this purpose of assimilation that they simply utter one mantra: "Resistance is futile." Regardless of your efforts, eventually you will be assimilated.

Unfortunately, The Borg's way of operating is similar to a parenting model that many of us grew up with and, even more unfortunately, that many of us continue to practice today. You've heard it before, maybe even out of your own mouth: "You have a rebellious streak, young lady, and it's my job to break you of it and mold you into [fill in the blank]." This is ultimately parenting by assimilation, whereby parents *need* to exercise their power to bring all the children into line in order to feel in control of the family.

In my therapy and coaching practice, I see this type of family system all the time. And whenever I see this type of arrangement in a family, I know one thing for sure: The parents feel threatened. They are unsure about their position of influence, and they feel intimidated by a child's exertion of will. So the parents step up their use of power to counter the child's. Here's where many familiar "power struggles" occur. When a child does not show an act of willfulness, then the parents assume she is fine, and they do not feel threatened. Thus they do not need to exert themselves. What this dynamic leads to is a relationship based mainly on power struggles with little room for connection off the battlefield.

Far too often, the only way these parents connect to their children is by bringing them into the fold whenever they challenge the status quo. If there is no challenge, then the parents' anxiety is reduced and things remain relatively calm. If there is no challenge, however, there is no connection. That's the real tragedy here. As a child in this family, you are either the rebellious one in need of constant attention or the "lost child," the one "we never have to worry about." Both of those options will create a difficult journey for the child (and parent) in the years ahead.

ScreamFree Parenting offers a different way. Ironically, it employs the same phrase The Borg uses: "Resistance is futile." The difference is that instead of saying it to our kids, we say it to ourselves.

Throwing Down the Gauntlet

As I mentioned before, when children exert their will, most parents view it as a direct challenge to their authority. How many times have we heard this well-meaning phrase in parenting magazines and radio talk shows: "Whenever children challenge you, you've got to pick your battles."

Listen to the language. The sentence assumes that the exchange between you and your child will be a hostile one in which there is a triumphant victor and a vanquished foe. This type of rhetoric assumes that the challenge issued by your child is just that—an invitation to battle. Instead, I'd like to offer a different word and a radically different idea. Instead of considering your next trying interaction with your child as an impending Waterloo, consider this: In your child's developing growth, he is constantly *testing* you. In doing so, he is not plotting an invasion or laying an ambush. Instead, he is testing you to see if you can be trusted. He is testing you so that he can see that you are dependable, stable, and consistent. And trust me, he desperately needs you to pass.

You might be thinking "You mean when kids push our buttons, they don't really want us to give in?"

Your child is testing you to see that you are stable and consistent. And he wants you to pass.

Yes and no. Yes, their anxiety wants you to cave at that moment, but their "inner adult" is begging you to not get ruffled and to remain calmly focused on yourself.

I know, so often this testing feels like a fight. It feels as if your kids are digging a trench and loading their bazookas. What they are really doing, however, is throwing down a gauntlet. In medieval times, the gauntlet was a protective glove worn by knights. When thrown down at the feet of an adversary, the gauntlet was an invitation to battle. Picking up the gauntlet was an acceptance of the invitation, an acceptance of the mutual responsibility for whatever happened next. And the same is true in parenting. When kids throw down a gauntlet, they are testing you to see if you are willing to take responsibility *for* them.

Children throw down a wide variety of gauntlets: "I'm bored," "Are we there yet?" "You're not fair!" "I don't want to do it and I'm not going to," "I hate you!" Can you recall what the pit of your stomach felt like the last time Junior uttered one of these phrases? Many parents find themselves reaching down, snatching up the gauntlet, and engaging their child in an all-out battle before they know it.

What does this have to do with The Borg? By employing the phrase "resistance is futile" when considering a child's emotional show of force, a ScreamFree Parent can instead use that child's own momentum to change the encounter completely.

Let me explain by mixing metaphors a bit. Judo, or "the Way of Gentleness," is a discipline whereby the momentum of the opponent, rather than raw, brute force, is used to change the outcome of the encounter. It is a model of conflict, if you will, that chooses not to pick up the gauntlet. In a conflict, the student of judo is still engaged with the other person, choosing to remain connected. But the participant is not going to attack the other or accept the invitation to fight. The judo participant is, instead, going to accept the other's momentum as belonging to the other, something not to be resisted. Instead, it is to be respected. Just listen to the words of Jigoro Kano, the father of judo:

> If one enters a contest with the sole idea of not being defeated, automatically, the body becomes stiff and defensive—and they appear to be entirely preoccupied with the idea of winning their contest, without any sign of aspiring to higher accomplishment. [Instead], the principle is to evade the opponent's strength or change one's position to *reduce the effect of the strength applied.*[1]

Jigoro Kano often spoke of the willow tree. He observed that in the harsh Japanese winters, seemingly stronger trees were losing their branches to the heavy snow while the supple willow tree simply allowed the snow to glide off its branches. The willow uses the weight of the snow and bends with it rather than attempting to overpower it. This approach to conflict necessitates a willingness to learn about the other, a willingness to carefully observe the other and his or her momentum. Only then can you know how to respond without directly resisting the other's invitation to combat.

You can already see the parallels between the judo model of combat and the ScreamFree model of relationships. Your children, through their own anxious efforts to handle their emotions and responsibilities, will try to engage you in a test. Think of the two-year-old deliberately picking up a forbidden object, immediately after you told him not to, while looking devilishly at you the entire time. Think of the school-age girl screaming that you're the worst mommy in the world because you won't let her do "what everybody else" does. Think of the teenager; enough said.

Your children, through their own anxious efforts to handle their emotions, will try to engage you in battle.

These are all tests, tests that only become "battles" when we take responsibility for our child and pick up the gauntlet.

Refusing to Pick Up the Gauntlet

ScreamFree Parenting offers another way altogether. Remember, judo is the art of going with another's momentum. So the ScreamFree parent asks, "How can I employ my children's desires for motivation, connection, and discipline? How can I bend like the willow tree when they throw gauntlets at my feet?" Let's explore the ScreamFree possibilities with some common tests.

"I'm bored."

This is the classic gauntlet. And so often we are quick to pick it up. First, we get angry. "Bored? How could you be bored? Why don't you go play upstairs with all of those toys I bought you?" "You know what's boring? Working my job every day to buy you those toys, that's what's really boring."

Then we get anxious. "You mean you can't find anything to do?" We might even think to ourselves, "Is this kid totally uncreative? What have I done wrong?" Finally, we overcompensate. "Look, you could go outside and find Jimmy, or you could go upstairs, or you could do this, or you could do this, or this, or this, or this . . ."

A ScreamFree response could choose, instead, to never pick up the gauntlet in the first place. "Wow, you're bored? That stinks. I hate it when I'm bored. What are you going to do about it?" No resistance, just go with the momentum and actually join right alongside your child as she faces her *own* dilemma.

"Are we there yet?"

Another classic. You've been in the car less than ten minutes, and the complaints from the backseat have already started. And you've got another two hours to go! What is the typical, anxiety-driven response? To pick up the gauntlet, of course. "No, we've got an hour to go (we lie, of course, to make it sound better), so just sit tight and be patient." Now the battle has begun. "A whole hour?!? I'm never gonna make it!

You never said it would take that long. How long is an hour anyway? I'm so bored already." And they don't even know it's actually going to take twice that long!

A ScreamFree response could choose, instead, to never pick up the gauntlet in the first place. "Wow, you're already asking that question? You must really not want to be in the car today." Empathy. "Come to think of it, I don't want to be in the car either. And I really don't want to be in the car for a whole two hours either. I think I want to be out of the car more than you do! What do you think?" By joining with your child, you can commiserate together (and actually have a fun time doing it).

**A ScreamFree Parent never picks up
a gauntlet in the first place.**

"Mommy, I can't do my homework."

A woman called me wanting to come to one of my seminars. Her objection wasn't the time, or the location, or even the price. Her objection was what she would do with her children. I told her we had babysitting available. "No, that's not it. You see, I need to make sure my husband can make sure our daughter does her homework." That's the type of statement a parent (and spouse) makes when anxiety is driving the boat.

She ended up coming to the seminar. You can imagine our conversation afterwards. She picked up on the irony. "So, Hal," she said, "if I understand correctly, I was saying 'I don't know if I can come to a seminar to focus on my parenting, because that would mean taking my focus off my child.

And if I have to take my focus off my child, then I need my husband to do it for me.' " I loved what she said next: "But you know what? The times in the past when I just couldn't be there to watch over her homework, she's done just fine."

Homework hovering is a major epidemic around the world. It serves as a wonderful microcosm of everything we're talking about in this book. The homework hoverer is saying, "I'm responsible *for* you, son, so I need to make sure you do all the work you're supposed to do. And since you cannot do anything else until it gets done, then I can't get anything else done either. So we're going to work on this together, making sure you get it done and get it done right." What is difficult for the hoverer to see is that the very act of hovering makes the problem worse. The child's motivation is now completely confused because it's now about keeping Mom or Dad sane, easing the parent's anxiety.

The child's unconscious thought becomes "The thing between me and getting to play with my friends is not really the homework, it's Mom's anxiety. Well, that stinks, because when Mom gets anxious it becomes more difficult to concentrate, more difficult to stay focused, and more difficult to think my own thoughts."

You cannot orbit around your child without giving her the distinct impression that the world revolves around her. And then you act surprised when she acts both selfish and incapable. Homework hoverers forget whose homework it really is. As you learn to calm your own anxiety about her performance, you do not have to pick up this gauntlet. "So, you've got a tough one there, huh? I hate it when I can't figure something out. What are you going to do about it? Who can you call in your class that could help you?"

> ## You cannot orbit around your child without giving her the impression that the world revolves around her.

Children's school work is *supposed* to make them struggle. It is *designed* to be difficult for them. That's the whole point! Helping them too much with it would be like lifting weights for them and then wondering why they're not building any muscle! Calm yourself down and let them struggle. Let them invite you alongside to help them through the struggle but do not try to "be there for them." You can't. It's their problem, not yours.

"I hate you!"

Allow yourself to feel this one. What emotional reactions come to the surface? What do you immediately want to say?

"Well, I certainly love you, young lady!"

Or "How dare you say that to me after all I've done for you!"

Years ago, I had a client whose seventeen-year-old son, in a spiteful effort to communicate his anger and hatred toward his parents, decided not to open any of his Christmas presents from them. Not one present. For a full year they sat, unopened, in an upstairs closet. Now, that is a pretty big gauntlet. Mom was so tempted to pick it up by reacting emotionally. She felt so much pain she wanted to throw him out of the house, lash out at him every day, tear up his things, you name it.

She decided to focus on herself instead, asking herself some incredibly tough questions about her relationship with her son. "What's been going on that would lead us to this? What would lead a kid to act so spitefully, even denying himself material gifts just to get back at his parents? Is he just a psychopath, or have I been contributing to the pattern this whole time?"

With this pause, Mom could then ask herself the best question of all: "What can I do differently to begin repairing this relationship? And how can I do it without losing my cool, getting reactive, and simply making things worse?"

What's great about the ScreamFree path is that the second you want to get on it, you're already there. In this case, whatever decisions she decided to make with her son, from there on out, had the potential for positive change, simply because she would be acting out of self-awareness and self-direction. By simply stepping back and choosing not to react, she assured herself that her next step would not be reactive. And then she could choose her next step, rather than having it chosen automatically for her by the previous patterns of combat.

"I don't wanna do it, and I'm not gonna do it."

Ah, the sound of metal hitting the floor. Even as I write this, I want to pick up *this* gauntlet. "Oh yes, you are, young man. You're going to start showing some respect around here. I'm sick and tired of hearing you say what you will and will not do. You don't make the rules around here, mister, and it's time you started accepting that fact." If you haven't said it, you've definitely thought it, right? I know I have.

A ScreamFree Parent could choose another response. Choosing to focus on herself, the ScreamFree parent could pause and ask herself why this demonstration of will bothers her so much. "Why do I take it personally when he asserts his will? Do I feel threatened? Is he out of my control? How far is he going to take this? Am I raising the next Hitler?"

The irony is, of course, that the more we do take it personally, the more reactive we get to this demonstration of will, the more we encourage it. Emotional reactivity simply creates more emotional reactivity.

But again, the entire goal of parenting is to launch our children into the world as self-directed adults. We want them to be capable of asserting their desires, making their own choices, and taking responsibility for their actions. We want them to be able to stand up for themselves and choose for themselves what they will and will not do. We just don't like it when they practice demonstrating that will *on us*.

"Sure, I want him to say no to his buddies when they want him to try smoking pot, but I sure don't want that attitude with me when I tell him to come inside!"

Our goal is not to *stifle* our children's expressions of will, desire, and emotion. Our goal is to help *steer* those expressions along the most productive paths. As you learn to keep your cool, you can see this defiant stance as yet another gauntlet, and you can choose not to pick it up. "You're not going to come inside, huh? I guess you really don't want to, because you usually don't talk like that to me. I'm going to let you think about that for a few minutes."

Your goal is not to stifle their emotions but, rather, to steer them toward productive expression.

After a few minutes, you return to offer him a choice: He can come inside or face a consequence. And it's totally his choice.

"Well, you're not the boss of me!" may come his response. Another tempting gauntlet.

"You know what, son, you're right. I'm *not* the boss of you. You are. And as the boss, you've got a choice to make: You can come inside in the next two minutes, or you can lose TV for the next two days. It's your choice."

Why *Should* Our Children Obey Us?

Now let's ask ourselves a very tough question: Why *should* our children obey us? What in the world is their motivation? Is it to please us? How long do you want that? Not very. What we want is for them to do it for themselves. We get frightened when we don't see them operating from their own motivation.

So why in the world *should* my son obey me? Because I said so? Because he should respect my authority? Because he needs to learn to obey his elders? "He should do it just because it's the right thing to do!" Right? Yes, yes, yes, and yes, from our perspective. But that's not *his* perspective. Why, from *his* perspective, should he obey? What's in it for him? What is his motivation for coming inside, or going to school on time, or turning in his homework? Why should he do any of this?

As long as the only answer I can give to this question is from my perspective, then I am simply inviting a losing power struggle. As long as I can only answer what I think his motivation should be, and that motivation is "because it's the right thing to do," then I am really saying that his motivation should be the same as my own. And I *need* him to obey because I don't know what to do if he won't. I don't know how to relate to someone who doesn't automatically want to do the right thing or doesn't want to please me. But that sounds like "responsible *for*" thinking, and we now know where that takes us.

So, in order to adopt the "responsible *to*" model instead, we need to start asking ourselves some more questions: What motivates our children? What do they really want? What *questions* can we ask that will help them discover and explore those desires instead of picking up their gauntlets and going head-to-head?

Doing this takes changing your thought patterns, I know. Initially this can be tough stuff. And I'm not promising you that it will eliminate conflict in your home. But part of changing your thinking should include the way you think about conflict in the first place. Consider one last quote from Dr. Kano:

> Before and after engaging in a match, opponents bow to each other. Bowing is an expression of gratitude and respect. In effect, you are thanking your opponent for giving you the opportunity to improve yourself.[2]

Be the first to bow to your children. Not out of deference, but out of respect and gratitude. Hopefully one day they will bow in return, but even if they don't, you will have grown. And that's what ScreamFree Parenting is all about.

I leave you with a letter I received from a parent of three

children, ages four, two, and three months. Listen to her as she comes to understand the value of practicing judo parenting.

Dear Hal,

I'm writing to thank you for your help with my four-year-old. She is going through a bout of negativity and frustration lately that I haven't been able to find a cure for. The other day, we wasted more than an hour of our day when she broke down trying to write the number two. She traced it and then looked up pouting and said, "Mommy, I want to write a two, but I can't do it."

"Would you like me to make dots that you can trace?"

"No."

"Would you like me to help your hand write it?"

"No."

"Is there another way you want me to help you?"

"Tell me how to do it."

"Okay. Put your pen on the paper right here and . . ."

"No! I KNOW I CAN'T DO IT!" she screamed, and then broke down in tears. I was so frustrated.

Eventually, her tears turned into angry screams (which aren't allowed in our house), so I sent her to her room, all the time wondering if I was making the right choice (and feeling like a really mean mom). I wanted to hold her and tell her it would be okay, but nothing I did was making it better. And sending to her room just angered her more. The crying eventually stopped, and the number two was forgotten, but the day never really got better.

Then I read about your "Judo Parenting" concept. That's why I'm writing—to tell you what happened today.

Here we went again. My daughter wanted to play on the computer, and I told her she could after she changed out of her pajamas and into some regular clothes (it was noon). She went to her room and laid out the clothes she wanted to wear while I finished up on the computer. A few minutes later, she walked in and said, "Mommy, I can't get my clothes on."

Me: "Why, honey?"

"I just can't get my tights on."

"Do you want me to help you?" (We were about to reenact our "number two" day.)

"No!"

So then I remembered about the gauntlet and the idea of nonresistance. "Okay, honey. Let me know if there's anything I can do for you."

"But, Mommy, I really can't get them on."

"Okay, honey."

"But, Mommy . . ." She started to cry and walked to her room on her own. A minute later, she cried a little louder. But then two minutes after that (I was watching the clock on my computer), the crying stopped and I heard her call me from her room.

"Mommy, I think I figured out how to do it."

"Did you figure that out by yourself?" I asked, walking into her room.

"I did!" She was beaming. I couldn't believe it. It's later today, and she is sitting on her bed reading a book. She is much happier than yesterday, and so is her mom.

Thank you for your suggestions.
Jill T., Alpharetta, GA

Reflection Questions

1. Reflect for a moment on your childhood. How did your parents respond when you tested them? What could they have done worse in response? What could they have done better?

2. We've all repeated the mantra: "You've got to pick your battles." We do this because so often it feels like we're in a war, trying to get our kids to do what we want them to do. What's a more productive, more principled way for you to think about it?

3. What does is it look like when your kids test you? How reactive do you typically become?

4. How might your family change when you stop resisting your children and start going with their momentum?

CHAPTER SEVEN

You Are Not a Prophet
(and Neither Is Grandma)

Language exerts hidden power,
like a moon on the tides.
—Rita Mae Brown, author

There's something wrong if you're always right.
—Arnold H. Glasgow, psychologist

This is a chapter about language. No, not about reducing the use of curse words around your children (although that would probably be wise). It is about the power of your language to shape your world and the worlds of each of your children.

Remember watching your children as infants, wondering what was rattling through their heads? I recall questioning what my baby's thoughts could be. Since she had no words to attach to those thoughts, did she think in pictures or sound? I carefully watched the process of her learning those first words; those first sentences appeared seemingly out of nowhere. The next time you get frustrated because your children don't listen to you, think of this: How do children learn to speak with an accent? Kids are actually fantastic listeners from the very day they enter this world. They have keen ears with which to hear every syllable, every inflection, every tonality in our conversations.

It doesn't take long before they begin to articulate phrases that surprise us, utter thoughts that astound us, and repeat sentences that embarrass us. A woman named Cindy learned this the hard way.

When her daughter was three years old, Cindy took her on a walk through the park. There Cindy learned how well her daughter had been listening to one of her oft-repeated phrases. And of course, it happened at a ridiculously inappropriate time. It always does.

The phrase was this: "You must eat your vegetables or you'll get scurvy."

This anxiety-based threat was something Cindy told her daughter repeatedly, even embellishing it with a horrifying picture of what scurvy can actually do (not that she really knew, but she painted a pretty horrible picture anyway).

Well, that day as they were walking through the park, Cindy and her daughter encountered three people walking toward them. One had an unfortunate physical ailment that prevented him from walking normally. As they passed the group on the sidewalk, Cindy nodded a polite greeting and kept walking. Her three-year-old daughter, however, had something to say.

She stopped in her tracks, turned around, put her hands on her hips, and proclaimed indignantly, "He should have eaten his vegetables!"

Almost every parent has a similar story, some even more embarrassing. What this story illustrates is another way we shape the relational environment of our home—through our use of language. Linguistic experts have been helpful in teaching us how powerful we are as parents in shaping the very thought patterns of our children. Language is the currency of all relationships, including how any of us relate to the world outside of ourselves. It gives us vocabulary to express thought, grammar to govern our interactions, and stories to shape our worldview.

You are probably aware of all this. You've probably read or heard information about the language transmission process that has blown your mind. What you may not be aware of is how the words you use around and about your children actually shape their sense of space.

As we've seen in the last three chapters, keeping our cool helps create and honor our children's space, their freedom to grow into self-direction. By placing limits on our own freedom, we thereby create and honor theirs. When it comes to our language, especially the words we use about our children, we again need to limit our freedom. We simply do too much talking about them. Too much comparison. Too much categorization. Too much prognostication. And it's time to stop.

Becoming a ScreamFree Parent means taking a very hard look at our own anxiety-driven need to label our child's tendencies and predict our child's destiny. Before you think you may not have this problem, keep reading. Let's begin by looking at the power of labels.

The Power of Labels

All of us can recall countless stories of the power of labels. Even if they are innocently applied, they can become insidiously powerful. The truth is, labels are among the most powerful forces that shape our relationship with the world. Labels have the remarkable ability to stick far beyond their reasonable life span. I'm sure you've heard about two adult sisters still thinking about themselves as "the pretty one" and "the smart one." With two sons, it's usually more like "the athletic one" and "the smart one." These labels affect us all. Each of us could list several that hang on us like the stickiest Post-it notes.

Labels are among the most powerful forces that shape our relationship with the world.

Take a moment now to glance at just a few of the labels parents commonly use. Which ones have you been carrying around all these years?

Gifted
Full of potential
Funny
An underachiever
A little slow
Lazy
High maintenance
Laid-back

Strong-willed
Beautiful
Melodramatic
The one we never have to worry about
A bit of a troublemaker
Skinny
Big-boned
A hard worker
The star
The black sheep

Now, not all of these labels sound damaging, I know, but trust me, they can be. Did you see any that apply to you? If not, think about it for a second. Now say the label out loud. Think for a minute how much this label has shaped your opinion of yourself. How has it shaped your decision-making? Your career choice? Your mate selection? How does this label still affect you today?

The tricky part about labeling is that often these labels seem accurate. After all, they don't simply arrive out of thin air. Labels are typically based on some observable trait or behavioral pattern. For example, one year little Johnny, despite his demonstrated intelligence, did poorly in school. So, he'll always be "an underachiever." When she was seven, Suzy blew up in anger on a regular basis, so she forever has "a temper problem."

But hear this: You are not a prophet. Most likely you are also not a biogeneticist. You cannot predict how your children will turn out based on your own intuition or on your family's physical, mental, and emotional characteristics.

"You know, he gets his temper from his daddy."

What?! How do you know that? What does that even mean? Is temper a biological trait a child can inherit? Or is it a learned reactivity? The scientific community is still conflicted when it comes to answering these questions, but we somehow have knowledge the scientists do not?

"You know, she's gonna be a neat freak just like Mom was."

What?! Why would you pronounce such a curse? Just because your children demonstrated a certain pattern of behavior at one time does not warrant branding them with a label for life. And just because someone else—perhaps an aunt, a teacher, or a coach—slapped a label on them does not necessarily make it truth. We are so quick to judge our children according to small slices of life, without ever seeing a broader picture of the different possibilities.

Whenever we label our children, we severely limit their space.

I love the quote by noted poet, photographer, and legal guru Gerry Spence: "I would rather have a mind opened by wonder than one closed by belief." Especially the belief of an anxious parent.

Whenever we label our children, even in innocent recognition of certain characteristics, we severely limit their space. We risk permanently handicapping their future development. By labeling, we stamp out the wonder inherent in the childhood journey. But labels are not the only way of creating such a handicap and deflating a child's curiosity.

The Magic of the Self-Fulfilling Prophecy

I was four and my brother, Jay, was five. It was Christmas at my Granny's house. All the extended family was there. Jay and I were playing with our new Legos on the floor when something occurred to our dear Granny. She saw that while I was struggling to stack two blocks together, my brother was busy building the Taj Mahal or some monumental structure.

"Boy, Hal's gonna have to make a living with his mind, because he's sure not gonna make one with his hands, like Jay."

Now, this was an innocent comment, to be sure. My sweet Granny meant no harm by it, and the whole family laughed it off as a cute observation. Except the comment soon took on a life of its own. Sometimes it was retold for its own sake, but most of the time it had a reference. Anytime from there on out, what do you think was said when my brother did something creative or constructive with his hands? "You know, Granny always said that Jay would end up making a living with his hands."

What do you think was told at family gatherings every time I did something outstanding in school?

"Well, you know, Granny always said that Hal would end up making a living with his mind."

Here we are, over thirty years later. Do I even need to tell you that my brother has worked in several hands-on occupations (chef, vet's assistant)?

As for me, Granny wasn't too far off. I'm a family therapist; I work with other people's minds. Am I saying this is all

Granny's doing? Of course not. But there is magic at work here.

All of us can cite one example of a similar story with similar results. Although it's very difficult to determine how much influence such stories and labels have on us, we cannot deny one thing: They are powerful.

Let me say a word here about extended family. It's very important to surround new parents with support, but often this very support is a potential minefield of conflict. I once watched a new grandfather with his daughter and her first child, a six-month-old boy. The baby was fussy around feeding time and was not taking to the bottle of formula. The mother tried several tactics to feed her son without much success.

In disgust, her father barked, "I don't know why you don't just give the kid cow's milk. It worked just fine for you when you were a baby."

The new mother replied that it's been known for a while now that infants' stomachs aren't ready for cow's milk until a year old, but her claims went unnoticed.

"It worked just fine for you, it'll work for this kid," her father insisted.

So let's see. Since this new mother was a baby, we've landed a man on the moon, put a computer in nearly every home in America, and connected the world through an invisible network of technology, but we've made no advances whatsoever in understanding nutritional requirements of infants? Here's the difficulty: Whenever we choose any method of parenting that differs from how our parents raised us, we risk indicting them and their effectiveness as parents.

Yes, *A ScreamFree Guide to Leaving Mom and Dad* is on its way. And yes, *ScreamFree Grandparenting* is in the works as well. Until then, know this: People love to categorize, compare, and contrast. For some reason, it helps parents and their extended families feel as if they *know* their children. And we love to *know* our children. After all, what kind of parents would we be if we didn't? We've weathered the storms of the dinner table and the bedtime blues.

So, as they venture out into the world, say for a sleep-over, we arm the unsuspecting family with a list.

"They're finicky, you know," we warn.

This list may include sleeping habits, the order of bed-time rituals, and an extensive list of their favorite foods. When they come home saying all went well and they even ate green beans for dinner, we find ourselves putting them back into place: "But you don't like green beans!" As if their palates are already determined; as if we are the gatekeepers to any new preferences.

Why do we do this? Because in our anxiety, we love to prophesy, to categorize, and to label. It helps us give some structure to our world. It helps us to feel involved, on top of things, and capable of handling whatever unknowns lie around the corner. But what does it do to our children?

Are All Labels Damaging?

Here's a radical idea for you: What you say *about* your kids is more important than what you say *to* them. Sounds strange, but it's true. In this light, how powerful do even seemingly harmless phrases such as "Daddy's girl" and

"Momma's boy" become? Think for a second about the implied meanings behind such phrases. "Daddy's girl"? Really? Does he own her? Will she continue to be "his" when she becomes a teenager, an adult, a spouse, a parent? When does she become her own? Does she ever? And let's take a look at "Momma's boy." How do you suppose that would affect a boy's sense of self or masculinity? We may toss these labels around in all innocence and affection, but they hold incredible power in the lives of our families.

What you say *about* your kids is more important than what you say *to* them.

Think about some of the labels we mentioned earlier: funny, say, and hardworking. These don't sound like such bad qualities to have. Well, they're not. In fact, they are great qualities; they are also horrible labels. Why?

Your child overhears you say "Megan is such a clown all the time. She's always making us laugh and really livens things up around here."

If Megan hears this enough, what she will learn is this: "My job in this family is to make people laugh. Even if I don't feel like it, I have to try my best to be funny. I heard Mom say so herself—I liven up the place."

Try this one on for size: "My Dylan is such a hard worker. When it's chore time, I can always count on him to set the pace for the other kids and show them how things are done." What happens when Dylan doesn't feel like leading the way?

What we do with any repeated label, no matter how positive, is eliminate our children's freedom to be evolving, developing human beings.

What we must learn as parents is to fight for our children's right to evolve. We must fight for each child's right to create his or her own uniqueness in the world. What a gift we give to our children by refusing to stunt their personal development by foisting some "personality" on them. What a gift we can give by stubbornly refusing to compare them with their siblings and not allowing extended family members to label or categorize them. We give them the gift of discovery.

The first place for this to begin is within ourselves, naturally. Think of how we brace for an explosion at bedtime simply because there have been similar explosions recently. We're already prepping for a battle when this ever-changing child may be in a completely different mood. I know this is incredibly hard, because you are so frustrated, but you must hold on to the truth that with children (as with the stock market), past performance is never a guarantee of future results.

Here's a truth to live by: *No one is ever always anything.* No one is ever always lazy or always smart or always defiant. Just because your teenager wanted money the last time she did the dishes does not explain why she's doing the dishes tonight. No good can come out of accusing our children. Just because your child struggled in school last year does not necessarily mean he will struggle every year.

Strategies for Success

Change Your Vocabulary

Changing your vocabulary is an incredible way to defend your children from the onslaught of labels. Take the harsh words "always," "never," "all the time," and "constantly" out of your vocabulary for good. Replace them with two more realistic and forgiving ones: "can be." You'll be amazed at the way this changes the very way you think about your child. By saying "can be" instead of "always," you are recognizing the propensity for change. And change is woven into our very nature.

Here's an example. The next time your daughter launches into a monologue about why her life is so unfair, resist the urge to say "You are always so dramatic!"

Instead, pause. Take a deep breath and state, "You can be really dramatic when you feel like it. It must be really tough to be twelve. I can barely remember being that age myself."

This small change acknowledges the inner thespian in your child, but it does not lock her into a "personality" where she loses her freedom to be different.

Expect Your Kids to Surprise You

Believe it or not, your kids are constantly searching for new chances to start new patterns. But since relationship patterns always involve other people, it becomes difficult to change the dance without changing dance partners. They cannot choose different parents, so it's up to you to change.

What that demands from us as parents is a continuous, persistent desire to expect them to change, to act out of their best character. By no means does this call for some pie-in-the-sky naïveté about their limitations; nor does it mean being lax in the face of continued behavioral patterns that cause problems. As we discuss thoroughly in the next section, there are consequences for those behaviors, and you must enforce those consequences with consistency. But you cannot let those patterns determine your feelings toward and beliefs about your child and his or her future. Despite limitations and mistakes in the past, we must continually fight for our children's best character to evolve, fight for their right to always, always change at a moment's notice.

Become an Advocate for Your Children's Evolution

Your children are works in progress. Their fates are undetermined, their personalities yet to be locked in place. Even their looks will change over time. You have to become a champion for your children's continued evolution. Doing this means refusing to allow extended family members to categorize or label them. It means stubbornly searching for their best traits and choices and singling those out as the clearest indicators of their capabilities.

It means, most of all, constantly checking yourself internally and calming your deepest fears that because of this or that pattern of choices, a child is going to become violent or depressed or ugly or unemployable.

You are your children's biggest influence, and what you think and say about them may shape them more than any other force in the universe. Champion their evolution and watch them grow.

Leave Your Mom and Dad

You have children of your own. You live and operate in an adult world. You are more responsible to more people than ever before. You are growing up. That means it's time to launch from the nest. I know, you don't live at home anymore, but that is only a matter of geography. It's been said that the umbilical cord is the most elastic material in the universe. The launching process is the most important journey of your life, and it is by no means an easy one. We've already looked at that in Chapter 4.

Your need for Mom and Dad's input should decrease as your adulthood increases. Now, I know this is a hugely complicated issue, and it's one that will be fully addressed in another ScreamFree book, but put simply, you need to be actively growing your relationship with your parents to a more adult-to-adult dynamic so you can parent your own children without still feeling like a kid yourself.

Know When to Say When

What we ultimately have to recognize is that our desire to understand and categorize our children's behaviors is really a desire for something else altogether. In reality, we want to show ourselves and others to whom our kids really belong. Therein lies the problem. They don't really belong to us. They belong to themselves. When we pigeonhole them into a certain pattern of behavior, we limit their ultimate potential. We limit their discovery. We take from them the one certainty in life: change.

So, learn when to say when.

Years ago, when they first came into the world, we gave our children names; let's stop there.

Reflection Questions

1. What label did you grow up with? How has that label continued to affect you and your decisions well into adulthood?

2. What labels have you already placed on each of your children?

3. How might your discussions about your children change if you absolutely refused to hang a label, prophecy, comparison, or curse around their necks?

4. When is the last time each of your children genuinely surprised you with their behavior? How did you react?

5. What would be different if you approached every new interaction with your children without an expectation of their responses?

Storytime

This story involves a man and his ten-year-old daughter both having to adjust to a terrible situation. Look for Robert's revolutionary decision to create space, calm himself down, and become more available to his daughter than ever before.

A coaching client of mine named Robert got divorced shortly after his daughter, Jessica, was born. He later remarried. His relationship with his ex-wife remained terrible, and his relationship with his daughter suffered as a result. Suddenly, Robert's ex-wife discovered she had cancer and soon tragically passed away. Jessica was only ten years old and had endured more than her share of suffering. Now she had to move in with her father and his newly blended family. To make things even worse, she had to start at a new school in the middle of the year.

Robert had his hands full already adjusting to a new wife and her children. Now he took on the challenge of embracing his devastated little girl and the mixed emotions he felt over his ex-wife's death.

He needed space and he needed to avoid intruding on Jessica's space. Father and daughter were both facing a difficult challenge to grow.

Jessica was strong, but even youth has its limits. The Friday before Mother's Day, Robert got a call from the school. The class had started to make cards for their mothers, but Jessica just sat quietly crying by herself. By the time Robert got there, she was inconsolable. He himself was gripped by a flood of emotions. He felt so much pain for his daughter.

And yet, to be brutally honest, he felt inconvenienced, even angered by this whole situation. He could have chosen to become bitter and resentful. Instead, he chose to grow.

This is how Robert was able to make one of the greatest parenting choices in history. Who knows where ideas like this come from? It doesn't matter really. What matters is that Robert and Jessica connected that day in a way they'll never forget.

Robert took Jessica out of school for the rest of the day. He called work and told them he'd be back in on Monday. Then the two of them went to Party City, where he bought helium balloons and permanent markers. They went to a nearby park, where Robert explained that just because Mommy died, there was no reason why Jessica couldn't still send her a Mother's Day card. They just needed to make sure the card could make it all the way up to heaven.

He showed Jessica how to write whatever message she wanted her mother to read on the balloons. The heartbroken girl wrote, "I miss you, Mommy. I love you, Mommy. I can't wait to see you in heaven."

When she was finished writing, they tried to estimate how long it would take the balloons to reach heaven. Then Robert set his watch alarm to beep in a few hours.

Robert used that time listening to Jessica, creating room for her to explore her own feelings. She moved from recalling her favorite memories of Mommy to venting anger at her death and all the changes it brought. This anger included having to adjust to life with Daddy, a new stepmother, and new siblings. All this change was just too much.

Robert could have chosen to become defensive when Jessica spoke ill of his new wife and her children. He could have objected when she talked about how much better it was when she lived with her mother. Instead, Robert chose none of these responses; he chose to remain calm and let his daughter explore her space.

Father and daughter were in a deep embrace when the watch alarm went off.

"Daddy, did Mommy just get her cards?"

"Yes, honey. She's reading them right now."

Robert wasn't a genius. He was a confused and conflicted man who chose to set his own feelings aside for a moment to help his daughter sort through hers. He was a brave man who recognized that his emotional process was not his daughter's business. As awkward as it was, he chose to be responsible to his daughter in that way. And he was able to revolutionize their relationship in the process.

PART THREE

Keeping Your Cool
Means Creating a *Place*

There is no such thing as "fun for the whole family."
—JERRY SEINFELD

A stand-up comedian tells this story about a hot Saturday afternoon. After working all day mowing the lawn, he walked into his house only to find it crawling with kids. He didn't even know some of these little people. It seemed every person under the age of thirteen in the whole neighborhood was in his house.

He was hot. He was tired. He was a little confused. What he needed was a good, hot shower. Not only would that soothe his aching back and shoulders, it would be a great way to get away from the chaos that was loose on the first floor of his house.

Soaked and soaped from head to toe, he could feel the

stress and tension leaving his body. But then he heard something alarming: the door to the bathroom swinging open. Next came the unmistakable sound of two six-year-old girls giggling. He was just about to tell them to leave when the shower curtain flew open.

There stood his daughter, pointing her finger toward the middle of his body and educating her friend.

"See!" she explained. "I told you!" The girls flew out of the bathroom in a flurry of laughter.

Kids need to know their *place*.

Space without *place* is chaos. You may have been wondering about this as you read the last section. Okay, Hal, enough about space. When are you going to talk about discipline? Structure? Setting limits?

I saw a commercial recently with a woman on the beach, shouting that she wants to be free of the constraints of time, space, and her cell-phone calling plan. SUV commercials suggest that with their latest vehicle, there are "no boundaries." The possibilities are limitless. There are no constraints on what we're capable of. We cherish these fantasies of unrestrained space.

But think about trying to live that way. Imagine the responsibilities that would come with unlimited space. Being omnipresent eliminates one of the longest-running excuses for not getting things done: "I can't be two places at once!"

Just as *space* refers to our relationship with ourselves, *place* largely refers to our relationship with others. When your space bumps into someone else's space, you discover your limits; you become a little more aware of your place.

The greatest conflicts in life—in all of human history—are the result of two people (or groups of people) claiming the same space simultaneously. When two kids are in the backseat of a car, they will sometimes draw a line down the center of the vehicle. "Better not cross over this line. Over here is my space." And they go to war defending their kingdoms.

Place lets us know where our freedom stops and someone else's freedom begins. Boundaries are both freeing and limiting. In fact, freedom without limitation would be disastrous. Space without place would be anarchy: no rules, no way to determine right or wrong, no means of discerning good guys from bad guys, no possibility of protection against predators, no way to order life at all. On the other hand, place without space has no allowance for free choice, emotional expression, disagreement, or exploration.

Boundaries are both freeing and limiting.

Using a metaphor I will explain in the next chapter, it is your calling as a parent to set the table for your children, ensuring that every child has a secure place in the family. This place at the table is where each child is accepted as an individual yet expected to act as a member of the family system.

The truth is that you are already setting this table, one way or another, by how you set the emotional tone of the family's interactions. The question is this: Will you set the tone with your anxious reactivity, or will you set the tone with your principled decisions?

CHAPTER EIGHT

Parents Set the Table by Setting the Tone (and Vice Versa)

Ask your child what he wants for dinner
only if he's buying.
—Fran Lebowitz, author

My mother's menu consisted of two choices:
take it or leave it.
—Buddy Hackett, comedian

I f you were to ask your kids to describe their ideal home life, you might expect something like this: "Getting to do what I want, when I want, for however long I want." Sounds a lot like vacation. Vacation is great, isn't it? Getting up when you want, wearing pajamas until noon, eating Cheetos instead of Cheerios for breakfast. It's a chance to take a break from the mundane and just indulge. The kids love it. We love it—for about three days. Then we all start to get cranky. We start to get tired of the lack of routine and the abundance of freedom. We start to long for the familiarity of home and the comfort of routine. As adults, we recognize this.

Children, however, lack the wherewithal to understand that watching SpongeBob or MTV for five straight hours and feasting on Ding Dongs could actually start to make them miserable.

When children are given too little structure in the home, strange things happen. They choose to do what they want, when they want, and then get terribly frustrated when they find themselves unhappy.

Parents in this dynamic throw up their hands in disgust, thinking "Why aren't they happy? We're letting them get what they want!"

Here's something to think about: Children don't always want what they say they want. (Rare is the young child who says he wants a regular dinner with his family and a routine around bedtime. Even rarer is the young child who functions better without those things.)

Stability and structure are necessary components in a healthy home. This chapter is about your role as a parent in shaping these things for your kids. We have a responsibility *to* our children, a responsibility to set a *place* for each of them in the family. Often we think of this responsibility in a condescending manner, as if it's our job to "put these kids in their place." This type of anxiety-driven emphasis on punishment, even embarrassment, is not what I'm talking about here.

**Stability and structure are necessary
components in a healthy home.**

It's better to think of this as making sure to set a place for everyone at the dinner table. It is your responsibility to your family to set the table with calm, consistency, and commitment.

This means we're talking about structure.

"Structure?" you say. "What's that?"

Structure probably seems like something that happens in other people's lives. And believe it or not, there really are people out there who have structure in their lives. That's because these people have a good sense of *place*. They know where things "fit" in the scheme of things. In their family, it's an understood thing. Every family member has his or her place and knows what it is. They have clearly defined roles, an actual hierarchy in terms of authority, and a clear understanding of what choices are available and what consequences follow those choices.

The Two Sides of Parenting

In his book *Raising Children You Can Live With*, Jaime Raser teaches us to understand the dual nature of our parenting role.[1] There is a personal side to parenting and a business side. Under the personal heading fall such elements as fun, togetherness, nurturing touch, and play. These exist in special moments that draw us to our knees in gratitude and lift us to our feet with joy. They leave us dying to talk about our kids to anyone who will listen. Ever known a coworker who seemed to have a new story each day about the cute things his kids were doing? Ever been that coworker?

There is a personal side to parenting as well as a business side.

The business side of parenting isn't nearly as much fun. Under this category fall the basic operations of the family: setting schedules and rules, enforcing consequences, establishing curfews and bedtimes, and providing the basics of food, clothing, and shelter. And don't forget about supervising schoolwork and teaching how to clean those toilets.

Do children need to know they can have fun with you? Of course! Do children need to know you are the authority in their world? Absolutely. All of these things need to be done in order for the family to function in a healthy way. But how it gets done differs from family to family. Commonly, one parent performs the business side while the other enjoys the personal side. One stereotype is that Mom is the nurturer and Dad is the disciplinarian, but it can just as easily be the other way around. Sometimes the roles are not as clear-cut. Maybe Dad is a loving papa to his little girl (who in turn battles constantly with Mom), while demanding perfection from his two boys. Or Mom is best friends with "Sis," her eldest daughter, while tough as nails with her son (usually hoping to train him to be a better man than his daddy).

All of these manifestations are attempts to work out the

balance of the business and the personal—a difficult proposition, I know. One of the unavoidable truths about the way families function is this, however: The balance will work itself out somehow. It may not be the most functional balance, and it may leave one parent (or sometimes even the oldest child) having to do all the dirty work. What is most common is that the lines between the personal and the business get blurred beyond recognition.

This was the struggle of Jim, a divorced father of two school-age girls. He loved the fun times with his kids and he hated having to set rules and enforce consequences. So, in a very typical pattern, he would plead and plead with his girls to comply, all the while showering them with material gifts and lax curfews. When his daughters inevitably broke the rules, Jim became so infuriated that he would explode. "I give them so much and all I want to do is enjoy my time with them! Why can't they just obey me without me having to get upset like this?"

Jim would take it personally that his children broke the rules, and he would react by getting upset. Then, after his reactive explosion, he would feel tremendously guilty. In the end, he would allow this guilt to take him over, and he would back off any disciplinary action whatsoever. Of course, completing the cycle, his daughters would respect his authority even less and continue to disobey even the most lax of rules. In the end, the blurring of Jim's personal and business sides led to a disintegration of both, with very little fun and very little structure.

The ScreamFree Way

What ScreamFree Parenting helps you do is keep these two sides of parenting separate, leading you to develop the balance within yourself and within each parent. This means you can operate, with or without your spouse, with all the seriousness you need to establish order without sacrificing the joyful times and feelings you really crave.

Here's how it works: As you learn to calm yourself, it is far easier to operate out of your principles. And just as you teach your children, there is a solid principle about work and play. That's right—you cannot play outside until you take care of your chores. In order to enjoy the personal parenting times with freedom and love, you have to take care of the business side first.

Taking care of the business side means asserting yourself as the authority in the family. You set the table, metaphorically, so everyone—including yourself—can enjoy the nice dinner. This means setting your children in their place. Just as you recognize that kids need their room, you also claim your own right to privacy. You make expectations and rules very clear, in a matter-of-fact way, without any hint of anger or anxiety. Because you're already working hard to give your kids their space (as we talked about in Part Two), putting them in their place does not come across as an authoritarian power trip. You are a calm and connected authority, one who does not need compliance in order to feel like the leader, but one who commands respect and expects obedience.

Some parents gravitate all too quickly toward the disciplinarian role, however, in an effort to control the uncontrollable. By exercising their power over those dependent on them, they can mask their feelings of inadequacy and intimidation. This is not the ScreamFree way to provide structure.

"Setting the table" means focusing first on yourself and your parts in any and every developing pattern. Think about that for a second. If a behavior is getting replayed over and over again, it becomes very easy to focus on the other person, the one whose behavior you want to change. But here's the trick—a pattern always involves more than one party. And if you're experiencing a pattern with your child, guess what? Somehow you're contributing to the ongoing behavior.

What helps is focusing on your part of the pattern without blaming yourself or anyone else for the entire problem. It is a pattern, nothing more and nothing less. And all patterns can be changed. Just change one part of the pattern— yours—and the pattern necessarily has to change along with you. So, again, it is profitable to focus on yourself.

All patterns, no matter how ingrained, can be changed.

Jim, the divorced father of two I just mentioned, eventually learned to focus less on his kids' misbehavior and more on his own reluctance to set and maintain a clear structure. The more he began to set the structure, the less he found himself taking it personally when his kids chose to disobey. And the less he took it personally, in time, the more they respected him.

A perfect example occurred when Jim saw that one daughter's bike was left out on the driveway. Again. He had purchased the bike for her so that on the weekends she stayed with him she would have it available. And he was thus thrilled whenever she rode it because that meant she was enjoying herself even while staying at Dad's house.

But then she left it out in the driveway instead of putting it up in the garage. And she was leaving first thing in the morning to go back to her mother's house.

Jim was so tempted to feel hurt and/or explode. After he purchased the bike, he and his daughter had gone over the rules in a very harmonious way. She agreed to put the bike away every time in an I'm-so-excited-to-have-the-bike-I'll-agree-to-anything sort of way. But she seemed to leave it out every time, and Jim was left either to scream until he got results or take it in himself.

But not anymore.

After confronting his own fears of fully realizing his authority to set structure, Jim decided to stop his part of this pattern. He said, "Honey, it's obvious that you love your bike, and that's great. But you have left it out in the driveway. So I want you to know that whenever you do that, you have a choice. You can choose to bring it in to the garage, where it belongs, and thus keep it to ride next time you come. You can also choose to leave it out in the driveway, that's your choice. I will not be angry. I will instead choose to respect your choice. You need to know that if you decide to leave it outside, I'm going to take the bike to Goodwill in the morning."

Instead of quietly hoping that each weekend visit would just go smoothly, without any need for disciplinary consequences, Jim realized in both thought and action that *his* place is to calmly help his daughters know *their* place. That's what it means to be an authority in the home.

So what are some of the barriers to fully accepting and asserting your authority as a parent? What exactly is the anxiety most parents have to address when it comes to accepting and asserting their position of authority?

"Best Friends" Parenting

You love your kids. You love spending time with them, you love having fun with them, and you love those wonderful times of personal connection. Because of the intensity of these feelings, parents find it incredibly tempting to compromise their principles. As a therapist, I see red flags anytime I hear about the best-friends type of relationship developing between a parent and a child. This is not so much because of what such a relationship does to the kids. (It can do plenty of harm, yes, and many others have said so before me.)

Rather, I see red flags because of what it does to the parent-child relationship. This "best friends" type of relationship with their children is often an effort by parents to compensate for the validation they didn't receive from their parents—and what they're not yet able to receive from themselves and their adult peer relationships.

Parents are usually unaware of this process; they believe they are simply enjoying their kids and doing what's best for them. They love to spend time with them and absolutely cherish those rare close moments of connection and affection. This closeness is almost intoxicating, especially as the children age, because later these moments become so irregular and fleeting. All of us look for and hold on to those loving moments of kindness, fun, and yes, even friendship with our kids.

But what can this approach to parenting do to the family? When taken too far, it undermines the parents' attempts to set the table because they no longer have a position of authority. Once parents begin looking to their children to fill any sort of emotional need, the children can no longer look to the parents for stability and guidance. Seen in this light, "best friends" parenting is obviously counterproductive.

Growing Children Are *Supposed* to Want More Space

Now, you must understand that children don't have a firm grasp on where their space ends and yours begins. So, expect them to try to expand their space, enlarge their territory. They won't want to share right away. They'll keep saying "Mine!" like the seagulls in the film *Finding Nemo*. Your son will flip out completely when you all need to leave in five minutes and he has just one more level to go before rescuing the princess warrior. Your daughter will do the same when she needs a few more brushes to get her hair just right. They're fighting for their space, defending their territory, trying to discover the borders of their kingdom.

But, hear me well. I am not saying that you should let them run wild or let them act selfishly without any restraint. I'm saying just the opposite. Part of our responsibility is to provide our children with their own space by setting their place. This means giving them their room and letting it be theirs. It also means letting them know what is most decidedly *not* theirs. They're not going to like it when you set those limits, but fighting for their space is a normal part of healthy development. Fighting to increase their space in this world, their kingdom, is their job.

Children have the very difficult task of asking for us to provide structure while striving to claim as much territory as possible. Parents have the very difficult task of setting limits on their children's space while respecting their freedom within those limits. It's tricky, sure, but parenting isn't easy. It's an opportunity for challenging growth.

In their book *The Seven Worst Things (Good) Parents Do*, Dr. John and Linda Friel shed some light on this topic:

> Children need and desire structure. They don't know how to ask for it directly. In weak systems, they also get seduced by the lack of structure. They get used to it, intoxicated by it, and then they can't let go of the inordinate amount of power they have acquired. The ultimate dilemma for parents and children when it comes to this issue is that they both want to be liked because they love and care about each other and yet they both need structure. It surely isn't the child's job

to provide the structure and at some unconscious level, children know this. The result isn't very good.[2]

In other words, kids want parents to give in, but they also want them to hold firm. They are asking for two things at the same time. And in response to this quandary, it is our job to provide *instruction*. The very word "instruction" comes from the words "in" and "structure." Basically, it means "to put structure into." According to this understanding, instructing our children is not simply telling them what to do; we must bring structure into their lives. Sometimes kids resist this structure. Unfortunately, too many parents then "scream," either by blowing up or running away; they either repeat their instructions louder, or they give up and give in. Why does this happen? Because doing so is easier than standing on your principles in the face of adversity.

The Structural Act of Balance

Many of the cultural revolutions of the last half century have centered on rebelling against hierarchy. Citing the mantra of the 1960s, "Never trust anyone over thirty," or the more recent bumper sticker, "Distrust Authority," groups have sought to revolutionize society by challenging the structural status quo. And some of these challenges have altered society in much-needed ways; think of the challenges that ended segregation and those that champion equal rights for women. These challenges were healthy, necessary, and long-overdue corrections to the abuses of hierarchy, especially toward minorities and women.

But some challenges to authority have gone so far as to question the validity of any hierarchy at all. Since hierarchy is so easily abused, the argument goes, then the very structure of top-down authority must be discarded.

But again, this reactive stance throws the baby out with the bathwater. Just because authority is easily abused does not warrant discarding it altogether. The damages of having no authority, especially in the lives of children, are just as horrendous as the damages of abusing authority. What is needed is a *nonreactive* acceptance of hierarchical authority. What is needed is ScreamFree leadership, a type of hierarchy that appreciates its influential role with integrity.

What we are talking about here is balance, the only thing in life that can never be taken to an extreme. When it comes to providing structure for your family, balance is needed, for there are extremes that must be avoided.

You can choose to have a structure that is entirely too democratic, with no authority other than the consensus of all the family members. This style always ends up as a chaotic mess of anxiety-led claims to unlimited space. Or you can choose a structure that is entirely too autocratic, with nothing but extremely rigid, authoritarian rules to be followed or else. This style always ends up as a constricting mess of either reluctant compliance or desperate rebellion.

To illustrate, let us return to the idea of setting the dinner table. In the chaotic family structure, dinner is always up for grabs. There is no set time for dinner, and it is usually catch-as-catch-can. Although this structure makes for a seemingly "laid-back" atmosphere, it is really chaotic because everyone's appetites become out of sync and everyone's timing becomes haphazard. Snack times blend into dinner time and snack foods (those that are easiest to "catch") become dinner fare. What really suffers is family togetherness and harmony, the personal side of parenting we looked at earlier in this chapter. I am not saying that the family dinner hour is the only time for togetherness and conversation; I am merely using the dinner table as an illustration for the overall family structure.

In the overly rigid family structure, family dinners are not only mandatory, they are the linchpin of the whole family lifestyle. There is no room for playing a little longer outside in the long days of summer, there is no allowance for switching seats at the table, there is never a time to pull out the TV trays and enjoy a family show together. In this scenario, place takes so much priority over individual space that there is no room for discussion, disagreement, or individual preference.

Just because authority is easily abused does not warrant discarding it altogether. The damages of having no authority, especially in the lives of children, are just as horrendous as the damages of abusing authority.

What often happens is a confusing back-and-forth between chaos and rigidity. The family will go weeks without any routine. Then, when the anxious parent finally has enough, he or she begins to implement this new "from-now-on" type of rigid schedule. This anxious reaction never inspires anyone to change and leaves the parent feeling exhausted and unappreciated, not to mention hopeless. And it's what inevitably happens whenever parents lose focus on their own behavior and focus more on the behaviors of the rest of the family. They stop thinking about their responsibility *to* their family as the calming authority the family needs. And in this vacuum of authority, it is usually the children, the focus of the parents' attention, that end up driving the family boat.

I've been a firsthand witness to the sad situation of many families that allow their child to be the unquestioned captain of their ship.

Here's an example. Consider Mandy, a child who hated dinner. Not just what was being served, although she did balk at that, but the act of eating together as a family. When her mother asked her to sit at the table, Mandy blatantly refused. She insisted she was not hungry, yet she would ask for a bedtime snack only thirty minutes after the family finished eating.

By the time Mandy was three years old, she knew exactly how to get her way in all matters, not just those related to family dining. She had a great weapon, you see, and it was her fabulous set of lungs. All she had to do was utter a single piercing note, and family members were instantly brought to their knees and she was spared the "agony" of family dinnertime. The family came to see me because they felt trapped by Mandy's tantrums.

And they *were* trapped—but not by her tantrums. They were trapped by their own anxiety about those tantrums. I listened as the mother spoke of Mandy's outbursts.

"She just won't come to the dinner table! We've about given up."

I asked, "What's the worst thing that could happen if Mandy doesn't get her way?"

Immediately the mother replied, "We'd never hear the end of it. She would rant and rave until we finally gave in and let her watch TV instead. I just don't think I could take such a scene."

"So, you're telling me that the worst thing that could happen would be that a child would throw a fit."

"Well, you don't understand. She can really scream. She once yelled so loudly that she was hoarse for three days!"

Before I could say another word, the father interjected, "Wait, is that really so bad? Is that really worse than what we are teaching her by constantly giving in to her demands to avoid dinner? I mean, we can handle a little screaming, can't we?"

Silence filled the room. Our ability to calm ourselves down, even while our children seemingly go out of control, is the best way to set the table. Only then can we make decisions out of integrity. Only then, when we're calm, can we decide what appropriate consequence needs to be enforced in response to that behavior.

And that's where we're headed next.

Reflection Questions

1. What images come to mind when you think about "putting a child in his place"?

2. How much do your kids need to respect you in order for you to exercise your authority? What are ways you can act to earn that respect?

3. What family rituals would you like to implement? Which ones are you already doing that you would like to see continue?

4. What do you allow to prevent you from fully accepting your role as the one in charge?

5. Name a parent you know who does a great job balancing authority over and respect for his or her kids. What about that parent inspires you to find a similar balance?

CHAPTER NINE

Let the Consequences Do the Screaming

If I had to live my life again,
I'd make the same mistakes, only sooner.
—Tallulah Bankhead, actress

A life spent making mistakes is not only
more honorable but more useful than a life
spent doing nothing.
—George Bernard Shaw, playwright

As parents, we have within our reach the greatest and
most effective disciplinary strategy in the history of
the world. Let's make it even more grandiose. We
have at our fingertips the most powerful teaching method
ever devised or discovered. No, it is not military school.

The single greatest teaching and discipline strategy is a phenomenon embedded within the fabric of life itself.

Simply put, here it is: Our choices have consequences. Every single one of them. It is a bedrock truth in life.

You know about this on several levels. You've seen the ripple effect of the smallest drop falling into a lake, for instance, and you've heard the notion about the mere flap of a butterfly's wings leading to a hurricane across the globe. Every action we take has come in response to a million actions before it and therefore leads to another million actions afterward.

All of our choices have consequences.
This is a bedrock truth in life.

Do you know what commands the most respect in a leader? (Hint: It's the same quality that leads to the personal maturity of self-directed people.) The quality that commands the most respect is an ability to accept responsibility for one's actions, regardless of the factors leading up to those actions. This is what we all want for our kids.

We want our children to see their spot in the world and be aware of all the influences on their choices. And in light of all that, we want them to take personal responsibility for their choices and accept with dignity the repercussions, the consequences of those actions. You make a choice, you accept the consequences of that choice—good or bad. That's the type of maturity we want for our children. That's the self-direction we've been talking about.

Well, here's the good news and the bad news. Good news: As I stated earlier, the primary vehicle for nurturing that type of maturity in your child is at your very fingertips. It is bigger than you, more powerful than you, and it is always ready for action. You want your children to grow up and accept the consequences for their actions? Then all you have to do is welcome those consequences into your home. It's really that simple.

Here's the bad news: If you start to welcome consequences into your home, first you have to learn to accept those consequences for yourself. And we humans have been avoiding those consequences since the beginning of time. By choosing to read this book, you have proven that you are willing to accept the consequences of your actions. You are already growing in that ability. But now it gets even tougher: You have to learn to watch your children suffer through their own consequences.

The Truth About Consequences

Marianne, a single mother of four, was engaged in a frustrating pattern with her fourteen-year-old daughter, Julia. Seems that mornings were getting harder and harder for both of them. They lived within walking distance of Julia's school, but Julia preferred to catch a ride with Mom on her way to work. Every morning Julia whined and stalled, and Mom reacted by nagging and screaming. This pattern, not unlike one you may have enjoyed with your child this very morning, had been going on for a long time. And it was destroying their relationship. But one morning, instead of screaming and nagging, Marianne decided to focus on herself. She decided to stop her part of the pattern.

Here was her proclamation: "Julia, I'm leaving in ten minutes. If you're not ready to go, I'm still leaving. It's your choice whether you want to ride with me or not."

This was not a loud, boisterous threat, nor was it an anxious plea to comply for Mom's sake. Marianne simply stated her intentions in a calm, clear voice. In the process, she highlighted Julia's own choice in the matter.

You can guess what happened next. Ten minutes came and Marianne went. Julia had to fend for herself. The way Marianne tells it, she didn't even really think about Julia until she got the phone call around noon.

"Mom, what can I eat for lunch?"

"Don't you have your lunch money for the cafeteria?"

"I'm not at school, Mom. You left me at home, remember?" Her tone of voice reflected her attitude: very entitled.

"You are going to walk to school right now, Julia, and I will not write you a note. You will take an unexcused absence. You'd better go now so you don't have too many missed assignments. Bye now." And Marianne hung up. She didn't call back to check up on her daughter. Instead, she returned her focus toward herself and what she needed to accomplish at work.

Once home, Marianne learned that Julia did go to school and did take an unexcused absence. According to the school rules, that meant she would receive a zero on every assignment she missed. Good, Marianne thought. Julia would get to learn a lesson about personal responsibility.

Julia complained and pouted, but it wasn't that much of a protest. She was too excited about going to the homecoming dance the next night—a hugely important occasion in her young life.

And that's where the story gets really interesting. You see, although Julia was aware of one of the consequences of having an unexcused absence—zeroes on all missed assignments—she learned at school on Friday of another consequence: If a student has an unexcused absence the week of a school event, he or she is not allowed to participate in that event.

No homecoming for Julia.

You can imagine Julia's response. Wailing, screaming, anguish. Of course, she blamed Mom. Of course. Mom could have waited for her that morning. Mom could have written her a fictitious note the next day. Maybe Mom still could. Even Julia's older brother sympathized with his sister's plight. He was the oldest and, according to Marianne, he and Julia hadn't gotten along in years. Now there he was, carrying a sobbing little sister in his arms, pleading with his mother to intervene with the school.

Can you recognize Marianne's dilemma here? She was excited that she had finally held firm, refusing to give in to Julia's pleadings that morning. That had been a tired pattern, and she had finally decided to focus on herself instead of trying in vain to change her daughter. She had acted with integrity. Julia had decided to call her bluff but then refused to take responsibility. Marianne could have reacted the same way as she had previously—more nagging and screaming, then finally caving in—but she didn't. She chose to stop her part of the pattern, to stop acting as if Julia had no choice in the matter. Julia did have a choice in the matter, and that choice had consequences either way. With this realization, Marianne was setting Julia's place. What Julia did with that choice, what she did with her space, was up to her.

But now Julia and her brother and sisters (and her date!) didn't see it that way. They all wanted Mom to cave in and fix the situation, to do whatever it would take to help Julia escape her fate. They were all furiously screaming for Mom to intervene.

In the face of all this fury, here were the questions Marianne faced. Indeed, they are the questions all parents must face as they welcome choice and consequences into their parenting. Did the punishment fit the crime? Well, what was the crime here? Taking too much time to get ready in the morning? Disrespecting her mother's own time requirements? Choosing to stay at home when she could have easily walked?

Does Julia deserve to miss the dance? That's the emotional way of asking the question. And that's the way the kids kept asking it.

Here's the principled way: Is missing the homecoming dance a natural or logical consequence of Julia's choice? The school believed so. And that's the real issue here.

Consequences are *not* just the domain of parents. The consequences for our kids' choices are not just in our hands; as our kids get older, consequences belong more and more in the hands of other authorities. This case was not entirely within Marianne's jurisdiction.

Here is where it is important to learn Roger Allen and Ron Rose's "inoculation" theory about consequences. In their book, *Common Sense Discipline*, they wisely ask us to remember how people become immune to polio—we each take a small dose of polio.[1] The same is true with consequences. The more our children are exposed to the small consequences of their small infractions, the less they will have to commit large infractions and experience large consequences. The sooner we can expose our children to the universal law of sowing and reaping (at whatever age they happen to be right now), the less they will need to have the larger consequences teach them as they get older. That's the idea.

The more our children are exposed to the small consequences of their small infractions, the less they will have to commit large infractions and experience large consequences.

As your kids get older, the realm of authorities they report to becomes larger than just Mom and Dad. And the consequences from those authorities become more severe. That's when you as a parent have to discern whether you can and/or should intervene.

For Marianne to intervene and interrupt the process, she would have had to compromise her integrity. Here's why. She would have to go back on her statement to her daughter. She would have to lie to the school and tell them Julia was sick. Marianne decided to ask herself what the consequences would be of her own decision. With either decision (caving in or holding firm), what would she teach her daughter about life and how it works? With either decision, what would she teach her daughter about their relationship? Most important, with either decision, what would Marianne teach her whole family about her own level of self-respect?

Protecting Versus Exposing:
The Real Struggle

We don't like to watch our children make mistakes. And we don't like having to take the time and energy to enforce the consequences. So instead, we scream. We threaten. We hope it works (meaning we hope our screaming forces them to behave the way we need them to). When it doesn't, we scream some more—and then our screaming becomes the consequence itself. This doesn't work, and we all recognize that fact. No one is learning or growing through this process, but what else can we do?

If you want to change, you can let the consequences do the screaming. You can learn to get out of the way and let the consequences do their job. How do you do that? Well, you can guess the answer: learn to calm yourself down. But before you do that, you must actively become interested in calming yourself down instead of focusing on getting your children to stop making mistakes.

Here's a question to help you confront your own anxiety: How do you balance protecting your kids from life's dangers with exposing them to life's lessons? Not only is this a tough question; I believe it is the most important question for you to constantly keep before you. The answer will change depending on each child, each situation, and each developmental stage, but the question itself never changes.

For instance, you're not going to expose a two-year-old to the consequence of getting hit by a car in order to teach him not to play in the street. But what about when he's seventeen? He'll be in the street all the time, behind the wheel in the most dangerous form of transportation on earth. And you can't be with him all the time. Sure, you could anxiously worry and pray he never gets into an accident or never gets a ticket. But remember the inoculation theory. The earlier he gets exposed to life's lessons, the less likely he will need the school of hard knocks later down the road.

But some of us give in to our anxiety so deeply and so often that we always answer the question the same way: I'm going to protect my children from every danger, even if it means denying them the experience of learning from experience.

I love the part in *Finding Nemo* when Nemo's dad laments losing his son. He says to Dory, the fish helping him find Nemo, "But I promised him that nothing bad would ever happen to him!"

After a wonderful pause, Dory tells the truth: "Well, that was a dumb thing to do."

Our anxiety tells us to protect our children at all costs. Do whatever it takes to ensure they make it out of our responsibility alive and well. Our anxiety tells us the worst thing imaginable is for our children to experience pain, so we had better do whatever it takes to avoid that—even if it means overprotecting them. Even if it means smothering them and never letting them out of our sight. Even if it means neglecting to enforce consequences. Even if it means helping them avoid consequences.

As a high school teacher at a college-prep private school, my wife has the privilege of working with some incredibly bright, gifted, and overachieving teenagers. The pressure is high for these kids, and for their parents as well. What never ceases to amaze her, however, are the lengths to which some parents will go to prevent their children from having to suffer clear consequences for their choices. Whether it is begging and pleading for an extended deadline or actually finishing a child's work, some highly reactive parents will do almost anything to prevent their child from experiencing consequences. The true irony is that, in the name of their children's education, these parents are denying their children the chance to learn. Learning from our mistakes is the most effective form of education possible.

I recently heard a story about a father who obviously could not stand the thought of his son having to learn through suffering. His son had a reputation, even among his friends, as a reckless driver. After one more ticket, a speeding violation for going 75 mph in a 35 mph zone, the son's license was surely in jeopardy. That's when Dad's anxiety took over.

Turns out Dad was a judge, and he decided to use his influence to "make the ticket go away." This kid's friends now say he's driving worse than ever. They're actually afraid to ride with him, and they fear he's going to kill somebody.

Calming Our Anxiety While Watching Their Mistakes

I think Billy Joel said it very well in his song "You're Only Human": Mistakes, in the end, are the only things we can truly call our own. There is a certain dignity in learning from our choices. We made the choice to stay out late, and we now get the experience of getting grounded as a result. There is a sense of pride there.

But most of us would love it, absolutely love it, if our children could learn without making mistakes. Think of how appealing that is. They would always act wisely, they would never have to go through the pain and anguish of tough lessons, and they would absolutely love and respect their parents' wisdom and experience. Therefore, we would never have to console them when we want to strangle them, we would never have to enforce restrictions that actually restrict us, and we would never have to watch our children make the same mistakes we did. And that last part is huge. How many times have we heard (or said!) these two sentences:

I don't want my kids to make the same mistakes I made.

I just want my kids to have some respect for my wisdom and experience.

The desires these sentences reflect are among the top desires of all parents, particularly those trying to raise teenagers. It is so infuriating for parents to watch their kids make a stupid decision that could have so easily been avoided! So many times, we know firsthand about the logical consequences of a particular choice; if our child just had sought our wisdom or listened to our advice, he or she wouldn't have to go through whatever's coming next. And we wouldn't have to go through it either.

Wouldn't it be easier if our kids chose to call before they came in late? Wouldn't it be wiser to ask us for help before they tried to fix the overflowing toilet? Wouldn't it have avoided all this unnecessary pain if they would have just turned in their homework on time? We could have avoided all of this!

Calming ourselves down while we watch our children make poor choices is about as difficult as it gets. It's also our most important task if we are to retain any influence in our relationships with our kids. What happens when they do stupid things or make stupid mistakes? We panic. We get reactive. We scream. And remember, what we're screaming is—regardless of the words coming out of our mouths—CALM ME DOWN! I can't handle what you've done, and I can't handle the fact that now I'm going to have to clean up your mess!

But think for a moment about where you want to be when your children make a mistake (and they consistently will). Where do you want to be in relation to them? Do you want to be standing *over* them, waiting for them to admit their mistake, show remorse, and acknowledge you were right? That's where you are whenever you need to say four of the most damaging words in any relationship: "I told you so." And then we complain when our kids won't talk to us about their problems or lie to us about their choices. No wonder.

Where do you want to be when your child makes a mistake?

But perhaps you want to choose to be somewhere else in relation to them. Perhaps you choose the other extreme position, *under* them. This is when you choose to help them escape the consequences, whether actively (fighting the school) or passively (neglecting to enforce your own house rules). You are beneath them, hoping they learn by the close call they avoided and hoping they never do that again. And then you complain that they don't respect you or ever come to you seeking wisdom. Why should they? You're beneath them! They come to you only seeking rescue. No wonder.

Choosing to welcome consequences in your home enables you to take a different position altogether. When you choose to welcome consequences, you choose to become a life guide for your children, walking alongside them as they struggle and suffer. You position yourself as a leader who operates in reality. You recognize that the law of sowing and reaping is bigger than you, bigger than your child's emotional explosions, and bigger than your anxiety.

That's the position Marianne, the single mom we looked at earlier, decided to occupy. She chose to stay calm, stay committed to her decision, and stay connected to her daughter through the painful process. Even as Julia wailed with anguish and seethed with contempt, Marianne remained ScreamFree. She did not preach, she did not blame, she did not tell Julia to calm down. Instead, she spoke with calm clarity about her position, her own hurt for Julia's situation, and her availability if Julia wanted to talk, or just cry. She even offered to take Julia and her date to the movies in lieu of the dance.

Consequences are a constant source of truth, experience, and education. They often hurt and lead us to feel pain, embarrassment, and regret. But they are here to help us, and they are available to help you raise your children.

Reflection Questions

1. How do you balance protecting your children from life's dangers with exposing them to life's lessons?

2. Recall an instance from your childhood when you learned a difficult lesson by walking through the consequences of your actions. What did you learn? Who was there with you, helping you to walk through it?

3. What are some mistakes you would actually *like* to see your child commit? Why? What might he or she learn from the experience?

4. What mistakes would you like to see your child avoid at all costs? Why? How anxious do you feel at the very thought of these mistakes?

5. For you, what is the hardest part about enforcing consequences?

CHAPTER TEN

Empty Threats Are
Really Broken Promises

*To what extent are children "spoiled" by material gifts
and to what extent are they spoiled by their parents'
failure to make them responsible for the consequences
of their own behavior?*
—EDWIN H. FRIEDMAN, *Friedman's Fables*

On my daughter's next birthday, my family is getting a dog. I know this for a fact. This is not a prophecy, and it is not idle speculation. This is ironclad, 100-percent guaranteed fact.

How do I know this to be true?

On that day, my daughter will turn eleven years old, and in our family, "We keep our promises."

It seems a few years ago, "someone" promised a pleading

little girl that "when you're old enough to help take care of it," we would add a canine to the family. I say "someone" because I like to think it was my wife who made this promise. That way I can blame her when the beast poops in the living room. But no, it was me.

Now, maybe this promise to a little girl was made after long sessions of careful planning, after hours of deliberate conversation between her parents, and after clear consideration of all possible ramifications.

Yeah, right.

More likely it came as a promise uttered in haste, in an attempt to deal emotionally with an anxious situation. "When you're old enough" is a great way to put off the inevitable or assuage the tears of a beautiful little girl.

So, since this idle promise was offered in haste and so far in advance, I can easily back out, right? I mean, we don't have the space for a dog, or we don't have the right backyard, or I can't be held to a promise I had to make just to avoid breaking my daughter's heart. Right? Surely there's some way I can back out and still keep my integrity. I just have to blame my responses on the whims of a little girl.

No. We will get a dog next year, simply because it was a promise. And, as both my children routinely remind me, "In this family, we always keep our promises." We keep them even if they were made in haste, with little forethought, and done in an effort to emotionally deal with an anxious situation.

A Word About Communication

"But you promised!"

I guarantee you've heard those words at least once from each of your kids in the past year. And they usually hurt. Those three little words carry such pain and disillusionment.

Let's focus on that word "disillusionment." One of the processes involved in our kids' launch into adulthood is letting go of the illusion of their parents' perfection. When they are little, our kids have to hold us up as perfect because that is what they need us to be. It's a safety net. What they know is that all they need is provided (or not provided) by their parents, the All Powerful. Little kids need their parents to be big and powerful, because when you're as short as a two-year-old, someone has to protect you. Kids need to be able to trust their parents, trust they'll be able to slay the dragon in the closet or the monster under the bed. And they need to be able to believe what their parents say is true. If they can't trust their parents, their guardians against evil, what kind of a world is it?

Let's take a step back and talk for a moment about communication. I know, every therapist always wants to talk about communication, but I want to try to simplify the topic. All communication comes down to two parts: what gets said and what gets received. "What gets said" refers to the actual words spoken or written. "What gets received" refers to the entire message and its effect on the relationship between the parties involved.

When I make a promise to my daughter about getting a pooch, what gets said is the stuff about the dog. What gets received is the dynamic between me, my daughter, and the rest of my family. By holding myself to a promise, even a promise I may want to take back, I create a dynamic that far supersedes even the happiness (or misery) of picking up poop. By keeping that promise, here's what gets communicated:

- The world has a certain order to it.
- People are accountable to one another.
- Authority can be trusted.
- Words and actions have meaning and power.
- In this crazy and chaotic life, promises still matter.

And to a little girl, when her daddy shows all of this to her, what she understands is that *she* still matters. That's what gets communicated with every promise we make, hold ourselves to, and then keep. And all those critical life lessons get taught without ever having to preach any of them. Just keep your promises, and those lessons teach themselves.

Another Kind of Promise

Makes promise-keeping pretty important, doesn't it? Now comes another wrinkle in the quest to become and stay ScreamFree. As challenging as it is, the entire process I just described happens just as effectively, just as powerfully, when those promises are for something other than gifts.

That process and those lessons get communicated just as wonderfully when the promise is to enforce the consequences of breaking the rules.

That's right: "If you do that again, you will lose your Game Boy for two days" is just as much a promise as "When you turn eleven years old, we will get a family dog."

It comes down to integrity. It's very important for your children to believe that what you say is what you honestly believe and will actually do.

I cannot stress enough what unfortunate consequences—both long and short term—you and your kids will have to endure if they learn you can't be taken at your word. At the same time, I cannot stress enough how revolutionary your relationships become when your kids know they can trust your word no matter what. It comes down to integrity: meaning what you say, saying what you mean, and following through with what you promise. The sooner you begin to incorporate this principle into your very bones, the sooner you will begin to see revolutionary transformations. For instance, think about the difference it would make if your kids knew for a fact, from repeated experiences, that you never give second warnings.

**It comes down to integrity—meaning
what you say, saying what you mean,
and following through with what you promise.**

But not all of us are ready to be taken at our word when it comes to the business of setting and enforcing consequences. Susan liked to make big threats to her kids. She's a comedian by nature, and everything she says and does tends to be funny. Her husband knows it and her kids know it. This sometimes made their family life a true joy. But sadly, this tendency toward silly humor made it difficult for any of them to take anything Susan said seriously. How could they?

Once I got to witness Susan's effort to address her son's behavior. As this seven-year-old kept pestering his mommy, this is what came out: "If you don't stop, I'm going to saw your butt off with a plastic spoon."

This threat was received with peals of laughter from everyone within earshot (including me). I could only wonder how her kids differentiate between her jokes and her serious comments. Needless to say, this particular threat didn't have much of an influence on her young son.

Such comments are a subtle way of trying to avoid the business side of parenting—addressing serious issues in non-serious ways. Again, as parents, we don't like to do the dirty work and we wish we didn't have to. We get so aggravated that our verbal instructions aren't enough to modify our child's behavior that we resort to whatever means available.

For Susan, that meant using a humorous threat, one which had no serious weight behind it. She hoped the resulting laughter might do the trick. You can imagine the uphill climb Susan faced as she began to mean what she said and say what she meant. Her kids refused to believe her at first, and Susan struggled with giving up altogether. That's the way it always is when we start to change our part of a pattern. The others around us don't know what to expect, so they crank up their efforts to bring us back to the old way of doing things—even if the old way wasn't very effective. But Susan found out, as I'm confident you will, that patterns are just patterns, and all patterns, with our own persistent self-direction, can change.

Consider my client Thomas, who eventually learned the power of keeping his promises in order to change a pattern. But he had a different pattern to overcome. His part of the pattern centered on his reluctance to keep himself to his own promises. Thomas was having huge problems with his teenage son, problems so serious that the boy was placed on some major restrictions. All of the restrictions were appropriate and could have been effective except for one huge detail: Thomas refused to set a date or condition for the restrictions to end. When pressed, he responded he didn't want his son to hold him to anything. He didn't want his son to comply for a certain amount of time merely in order to get the restrictions to end. Here's the problem: The son had no idea where he stood. He was left feeling more resentful because his father would not hold himself to any stated condition. Talk about a power struggle! The father had the ultimate power, and the son had absolutely no tools with which to fight. He was left not having a clue about his place in the universe. Not to mention he was losing trust in his father's word.

Your kids actually want you to hold firm—how else can they grow to trust you, others, and the world if they cannot depend (sometimes begrudgingly) on your consistent follow-through?

The Power of Consistency

"What you reap is what you sow."

"You made your bed, now you're going to have to lie in it."

We love these expressions because they seem to reflect some bedrock principle of the universe. These and similar expressions can be found in all of the most revered spiritual texts and most studied philosophies. But these philosophies aren't applicable just to the one receiving the consequences; they also apply to the one responsible for enforcing those consequences, and that means you.

Remember that being consistent will maintain stability in your world. Being consistent makes it easier to remain ScreamFree. And in turn, remaining ScreamFree makes it easier to remain consistent. Here are four principles to help guide your way.

1. Don't ever set a consequence that is tougher for you to enforce than it is for them to endure.

How serious can you possibly be by grounding your teenage daughter for two months? Are you crazy? Do you really think it's possible to babysit her that long? What about taking TV away from your five-year-old for an entire week? What? TV is one of your babysitters! Do you really want to have that much more pressure to entertain him? When we overextend ourselves, caving in when the emotional pressure hits becomes much easier. And thus, we break our promises and we break the finely knit fabric of trust with our children.

2. There are no shortcuts to setting or enforcing consequences.

Providing consistent discipline for our children is always time-consuming, sometimes exhausting, and never done from afar. That's right, it's supposed to be difficult. Remember, nothing asks us to grow up like helping our children grow up. And seeking to discipline with ruthless consistency is asking yourself to grow up. It takes more time than you have available, more energy than you think possible, and more strength in the face of constant criticism than you think you can muster. But I know you can do it, and in fact, you already are. Reflect on the times when you have been consistent, when you have followed through. I guarantee you've been able to do it more than you think you have. Keep it going.

3. Choose only those consequences that you are willing to enforce.

At first glance, this statement may sound redundant. Or ridiculous. How can you choose something you're *not* willing to enforce? It's easy, actually: You let your anxiety choose it for you. Here's what I mean. I am not going to tell you whether to employ time-outs or spankings or charts or any other particular consequence. People constantly ask me about these different techniques, and my answer is always the same: What do you *want* to do? I know this sounds like therapy-speak, but I want my purpose for asking the question to be clear.

What you do is not nearly as important as *how* and *why* you do it.

What is your motivation for spanking? Look down deep,

focus on yourself, and honestly answer the question. Why do you want to spank your child? If you say you do not want to but you believe it is needed, then you are not acting with integrity.

ScreamFree parents never do anything they don't want to do. You are an adult, and you make every choice. If you spank without wanting to, then you need to focus on yourself some more. Why would you choose a consequence for your child if you did not want to choose it? Because he needed it? For what? Behavior modification? To calm him down? To show him who's boss? In order for any enforced consequence to have its desired effect, it needs to come from the solid, principled decision of its enforcer. If you're wishy-washy about spanking, that will get communicated very clearly. And here's what you'll communicate: I am at my wits' end here, and I do not know what else to do but resort to the most base-level power I have over you, my physical size and strength.

As you've learned throughout this book, what that really communicates is that your anxiety is driving the boat. And if anxiety is driving the boat, then you are not really in charge. A relationship can only take so many anxiety-driven interactions before becoming an anxiety-driven relationship.

So which consequences do you actually, authentically, *want* to enforce? I want to put my kids in timeout because it teaches them the type of pause that I'm trying to practice myself. Timeout also creates the space we need from each other. I want to take privileges and material possessions away from my kids because that teaches them to value such gifts. And sometimes, the consequence I want to enforce is simply telling them, with clear honesty, how their actions or words have hurt me.

Choosing consequences out of our integrity eliminates the whole this-is-going-to-hurt-me-more-than-it-hurts-you falsehood our parents tried to foist on us. Kids can see through our lack of integrity quicker than anyone, and that is enough reason to become as comfortable as we can with the idea that we can, and we should, enforce consequences we actually want to enforce.

4. Only choose consequences you are willing to endure yourself.

A coaching client, Dan, had a recent experience with a traffic ticket. Both he and his teenage son had received speeding citations in the same month. Dan was confused about whether to tell his son about his own ticket. This was his son's third in the past year, which would likely cost him his license for a few months. Dan was understandably upset, but he wrestled with how upset he could possibly be, given his own speeding infraction.

"I taught him how to speed. I should probably teach him how accept the consequences."

Dan was so tempted to rescue his son by hiring a lawyer to "make it go away," because a suspended license would upset the entire family schedule. You see, Dan Jr. and his two younger sisters all attend the same private school. And Junior had been driving all three of them to and from school every day. With Junior's license suspended, Dan Sr. would be the one to drive them for the rest of the year. That's a big disruption.

Thus Dan Sr. was tempted to rescue both himself and his

son. He found a lawyer who, for a large fee, "could make both tickets go away." This was incredibly appealing. Dan could avoid any consequences for his own infraction and could avoid having to drive his whole family around for several months.

But like Marianne, the single mom in the last chapter, Dan was starting to grow. His integrity would not let him make such a cowardly choice. Calming his own considerable anxiety instead, he chose first to accept the consequences of his own mistake, even taking his son with him to his own court appearance for speeding. He then walked alongside his son as he went through his court appearance.

All these practical principles are dependent on one thing: staying calm. Consistent enforcement of consequences is the single most effective application of authority in the parent-child relationship—but only if you can think through your decisions calmly before you make them. By doing so, you greatly increase the chances that those decisions will be sensible, realistic, and helpful in facilitating everyone's growth.

Stay consistent with your words, yes; but most important, stay consistent with yourself, even if it means choosing some discomfort and inconvenience. As for me, I'll be getting a dog next year and all the responsibility that dog ownership implies. And that's okay.

At least I didn't promise her a cat.

Reflection Questions

1. How well did your parents keep their promises and follow through on their warnings? What did their consistency (or lack thereof) teach you about trust, authority, and the ways of the universe?

2. When are you most prone to make threats you don't keep? What effects has your inconsistency had on your parent-child relationships?

3. What consequences are you the most consistent with on a regular basis?

4. How might your increased consistency improve your relationship with each of your children?

5. How does remaining ScreamFree help you stay consistent? How does staying consistent help you remain ScreamFree?

Storytime

This story involves a teenager, Lindsey, making the mistakes of, well, a teenager. Her actions are really nothing new. The response of her parents, Mark and Jennifer, however, was remarkable. Their choices display the incredible power of keeping our cool, and their family revolution is well under way.

Lindsey was thoroughly looking forward to her birthday. Not only would turning sixteen mean finally getting her driver's license (after a year with a learner's permit), but it also meant a ten-day trip to Europe with her favorite aunt. For all of her fifteenth year, Lindsey had eagerly anticipated the trip. She had also eagerly anticipated getting rid of her learner's permit and finally getting her own driver's license. As with most learners' permits, hers dictated that she could drive only with a licensed adult in the passenger's seat. Her parents' insurance went a step further, dictating that she could only drive one particular car.

As Lindsey's birthday approached, the European plans came into place. Ten days on the Continent promised for an amazing trip indeed.

A month before the trip, however, Julie had to make the phone call all of us parents dread: "Mom and Dad, I've been in an accident."

Arriving upon the scene, Mark and Jennifer remained calm. Their only concern was their daughter's safety. Once they held her in their arms, they could learn the details. Lindsey's boyfriend was driving his car with Lindsey in the passenger seat. He lost control and struck a tree. The car was mangled, but both kids escaped with only minor cuts and bruises. The police took down the details, and everything slowly went back to normal—until three days before the trip to Europe.

Racked with guilt and apparently growing more confident in her parents' calm resolve, Lindsey decided to confess. "Mom, Dad, *I* was the one driving the car. We lied to you guys and to the police so I wouldn't get in trouble."

What would a ScreamFree Parent do here? What type of emotional reactions come to the surface? What would you feel: Infuriated? Disappointed? Would you feel torn? On one hand, you might be impressed that your daughter confessed at all, and yet on the other hand, you might feel manipulated, knowing that with only three days before the European trip, canceling as a consequence would be difficult and expensive.

Mark and Jennifer felt all of these things, which left them feeling more confused than anything else. With an amazing self-awareness, they knew they needed to turn to principles more than emotions. They knew they needed to ask themselves that critical question: How do we balance protecting our child from life's pains and yet exposing our child to life's lessons? After much reflection, they finally made their decision. With the calm of a strong and loving mom and dad, they approached their daughter with nothing but well-wishes. They decided to send her off to Europe with warm embraces and hopes she would have the time of her life.

When Lindsey asked about the car and her license and all of that, Mark calmly responded, "We'll have plenty of time to deal with that when you get back. Now let's get you ready to celebrate your sixteenth birthday, Princess, by sending you to Europe."

While abroad, Lindsey's guilt occasionally crept up on her, and she called her parents in tears.

Resisting the urge to say "Well, you should feel guilty, young lady! Here we are spending all this money and blah, blah, blah," Mark and Jennifer spoke of nothing but their fondest feelings. They asked her about all she was seeing and doing. When she stopped and told them how sorry she was, they would just ask her to tell them more about Europe.

But what about when she got home? How long did it take them to lay down the law? Lindsey's parents decided to wait two full days after she returned before addressing the situation. They got her pictures developed, they looked at souvenirs, and they talked and talked about Europe. Then her parents set a meeting with Lindsey, and they had a long discussion about how to proceed.

Mark and Jennifer told Lindsey that she was going to inform the police and the insurance company about her lie. Mark had already spoken with a lawyer and thus was fully informed about the possible ramifications. Lindsey might have to wait until her eighteenth birthday to apply for a license, the lawyer said, and she might have to get another learner's permit after that. Mark and Jennifer knew this could all result in a major inconvenience for the whole family. But they also knew they would stand right beside Lindsey the entire time, helping her walk through the tough consequences with dignity.

You can only imagine what this has done for their relationship with their daughter. It has been revolutionary, to say the least.

PART FOUR

Putting *Yourself* into Practice

Our children are watching us live, and what we *are*
shouts louder than anything we can say.
—Wilfred A. Peterson, author

D octors, psychologists, and, yes, family therapists all
have a word to describe their careers. These profes-
sionals do not operate a "perfect," they operate a
"practice." This is not because they aren't excellent profes-
sionals; it is because they have such a profound respect for
the immense learning curve involved in attempting such
professions. These practitioners are just that, practitioners,
because the learning curve never ends—they never stop actively working on themselves and their work. They are always practicing, never getting to the point where they no
longer need to work on their game.

And that's what ScreamFree Parenting is all about—
learning to develop a practice. It is not about figuring it all

out or eliminating your mistakes as a parent. It is certainly not about developing the right techniques for every situation. ScreamFree Parenting is about continuing a path toward integrity. It is a way of learning to live according to principles, not techniques. It is a journey of constant learning and growing, refusing to ever believe that you've made it or you can't learn anything else.

I hope that you, by reading this book, have begun to listen more and more to your core principles and less and less to your anxious reactivity. That is the result of learning to calm down. In this section, you will learn how to best begin that journey. Although it involves focusing more on yourself, the blessings that come from this journey are not just for you but for all those around you. The types of intimate, enjoyable, cooperative relationships you crave are waiting for you along this journey. These relationships won't develop automatically, and they won't come quickly. But you are on a path that makes these relationships possible and all the more likely.

There's another helpful expression about practice. We often hear, usually in association with sports, that "practice makes perfect."

But it doesn't.

What is far more accurate to say is that "practice makes *permanent*." What you practice over and over again gets ingrained as a pattern, and bad patterns are probably one of the reasons why you're reading this book. Therefore, developing a practice is recognizing you are always, always participating in either the creation of a new pattern or the continuation of an old pattern. What's great is knowing that you can change any relational pattern by simply changing your part. Practice changing your part and watch the changes begin around you.

Finally, please look carefully at the title for this section. You might expect a self-help or parenting book to say something like "Putting the Lessons (or Techniques) into Practice." That is not the emphasis of this section, or this book. At the end of the day, this book is all about you, putting all of yourself into your relationships, particularly those you enjoy with your children. This is about seeing your parenting as an engagement of yourself with each of your children as a separate, growing person. ScreamFree Parenting is not a problem-solving or behavioral modification model; it is a growth model. And this growth model begins, first and foremost, with you. And you are already growing more than you think.

ScreamFree Parenting is not a problem-solving or behavioral modification model; it is a growth model.

I urge you to dive into this section with one vision in mind: Taking care of yourself is your number-one responsbility to your family. As I hope you will see, the best way to put yourself into the practice of parenting is to make sure you are operating as the most healthy self you can be. I believe this is the great news you've been waiting to hear ever since you became a parent—it's okay to want to take care of yourself as well as your kids. In fact, not only is it okay, it is the most important thing you can do to raise loving, responsible, and self-directed kids.

CHAPTER ELEVEN

Put on Your Own Oxygen Mask First

Self-love, my liege, is not so vile a
sin as self-neglecting.
—WILLIAM SHAKESPEARE, *Henry V*

I define comfort as self-acceptance. When we finally
learn that self-care begins and ends with ourselves,
we no longer demand sustenance and
happiness from others.
—JENNIFER LOUDEN, WWW.COMFORTQUEEN.COM

Fritz and Tami Miller, business partners and dear friends of mine, recently returned from China with their first child, Talia YuSe. The adoption process meant spending countless hours in preparation for the trip, in legal dealings with the Chinese government, and in the long but glorious trek home with their new little girl.

What they hadn't prepared for was the fact that eighty-seven other newly adopted Chinese babies and their parents would also be on the fifteen-hour plane trip.

Now, my friends made it home all right with no permanent damage, but I can only imagine the look on the poor, frazzled flight attendants' faces as they began to deliver their safety routine to the parents of eighty-seven adopted babies.

As the instructions began in monotone Chinese followed by monotone English, most people tuned her out. "Be sure your seat belt is properly fastened. . . . Locate the exit nearest you. . . . In case of an emergency, use your seat cushion as a flotation device. . . . In the event of a sudden loss of cabin pressure, oxygen masks will deploy. Place the mask over your mouth and nose and breathe normally. If you are traveling with an infant or a small child, be sure to put on your own oxygen mask first before assisting others."

Suddenly many of these new parents perked up. The familiar phrase takes on a whole different meaning when a young life is literally lying in your hands. The thought of this tiny being, completely dependent on you, struggling for breath, is unbearable at best.

And because of the anxiety of that thought, it is far too easy to miss out on the wisdom of the flight attendants' instructions.

Without proper levels of oxygen, our brains do not function as they should. Our judgment becomes impaired, and we are unable to perform the simplest of tasks. And yet if an airplane crisis occurs, what are we likely to do first? You guessed it: Most of us would panic and struggle like mad to mask our children before even giving a second thought to ourselves. But here's the truth about airplane crises—and about life in general—and this is the amazing wisdom from the airlines: If you're gasping for breath, you can't help anybody else.

You don't have to be in a crisis, however, to appropriate the wisdom of this statement for all of life. You cannot take care of your family unless you first tend to yourself. It's that simple. And it's vital to the health of everyone involved.

You cannot take care of your family unless you first tend to yourself.

What Does It Mean to Be Selfish?

Why is our natural response to avoid this thinking? I believe it is because we vastly misunderstand what caring for ourselves first really means. Most people interpret self-love as selfishness, an obviously negative trait.

For those in religious traditions, this seems to be an especially vexing dilemma. We get caught in a trap by thinking we are facing an either/or dichotomy. Either I focus solely on myself or I focus on serving others, particularly my kids, who need me so much. Either I ramrod my way through life, looking out for Number One, or I decrease so others might increase, even if I get trampled in the process.

It seems that taking care of others necessarily means neglecting ourselves.

In discussing this with a small group of parents recently, one mother put it this way: "If I take care of me, I feel like a selfish jerk, like I'm doing something very wrong. If I focus on my kids, I sometimes feel like a doormat, busting myself to please and serve yet feeling very unappreciated for all the sacrifices I make."

Exactly. That's the false dichotomy. That's the dilemma we all face.

"Sure, there's a part of me that would love to focus on me and my needs for a change. But I can't do that. I won't do that. It's just not Christian. Or moral. Or right. Right?"

Wrong.

Other cultures have a very different take on self-care. The Hebrew Bible and, later, the Christian New Testament, seem to take self-love for granted. One of the great commandments in those scriptures is to "Love thy neighbor as thyself." Our culture would be in serious trouble if we put this into practice with our Western way of "loving" ourselves. Think about it. What would it really look like to love your kids as *little* as you love yourself? Instead of packing a healthy food-pyramid lunch with a loving note tucked inside, you'd shove a half-eaten doughnut and a Thermos of stale coffee in their bookbags. What would it look like if you talked to your kids the way you talk to yourself after making a mistake? Most of us would berate them over and over, calling them names and finding it incredulous that they made the same mistake yet again. "You stupid idiot; how could you do that again?! You knew what would happen, but you did it anyway." Maybe some of us already do talk to our kids that way.

What would it really look like to love your kids as little as you love yourself?

So, what's the solution? Is there another way to think about it, another way to live in our relationships? Thankfully, others before us have wrestled with this question. One fellow struggler whose thoughts are particularly helpful lived about a thousand years ago. A French monk, Bernard of Clairvaux, seriously wrestled with how to balance our relationship with ourselves and our relationship with others. He wrote his thoughts down in a work called "The Four Degrees [or Levels] of Love."[1] His particular question was how to balance a love for self and a love for God, but I think it's extremely helpful in learning how to balance all of our relationships. Allow me to summarize his theory.[2]

First Level of Love: "I love *me* for *my* benefit."

According to Bernard, this is the most selfish and the most infantile of the four levels. The practitioner of this level thinks, "I care for my interests alone, and I am only interested in results that immediately and ultimately benefit me."

From a developmental perspective, this belief represents a necessary stage in our growth as individuals, whereby we learn the basic skills of survival. As infants we cry for food, for clean diapers, for comforting arms. This is natural and necessary. Unfortunately, most of us know a few adults who still function at this stage of development. And, honestly, most of us can recall many times when we ourselves have regressed to this stage. Usually this happens when we have so neglected ourselves that one day we snap and commit a remarkably selfish act that surprises even us. Clearly this is not the solution for a way out of the dichotomy.

Second Level of Love: "I love *you* for *my* benefit."

Bernard believed this level is where most of us dwell, particularly in our relationships. Someone stuck at this level operates like this: "I love you and care for you because I receive validation knowing I add value to your life. I love you because I need to in order to feel right, safe, strong, worthy."

In the words of Cheap Trick, "I need you to need me." I love you because of what our relationship does for me, making me feel valuable and necessary. It also gives me reason to expect you to reciprocate my efforts. Bernard rightly questioned whether this way of loving others can truly be considered love at all, given that it is based on a hidden quid pro quo agenda. It's the golden rule twisted inside out. Instead of "Do unto others as you would have them do unto you," it turns into "Do unto others *so that they might* do unto you."

This is, frankly, where most of us find ourselves in all of our relationships, particularly as parents with our kids. Think back on the mother's comment about feeling unappreciated for all of her sacrifices. Who hasn't felt that way? Who hasn't wanted to quit making all these sacrifices because they keep going unrecognized and unreturned? But do we make all those sacrifices in order to feel appreciated? Of course not, right? We make all those sacrifices because we love our kids!

If that's true, then what's behind our need for someone to notice? This is not about wanting appreciation, it is about needing *validation* for all of our efforts in order to feel like it's worth it to keep going at all. "If others don't appreciate all my sacrifices, then why am I still making such efforts?" It is because I'm stuck at the second level of love: I love you for my benefit.

Third Level of Love: "I love *you* for *your* benefit."

This brings us to level three. I believe this level is deceptive because it appears to be the highest level of love and the most beneficial to the world. "I am selfless in that I am here for you; I am here to serve you. I am here to serve you and my concerns and personal motives do not come into the picture at all."

For a variety of reasons, this seems to be the stated and understood ideal for all relationships. We hear it in popular phrases such as "I'll always be here for you" and "I'll do anything for you." We feel like good parents when we say to our kids: "You're the most important thing in the world to me."

Yikes! I don't want that type of pressure, do you? Especially if I'm just a kid. That's a whole lot of responsibility to carry around, the weight of being someone's supreme significance. The truth of the matter is that this level of love, while sounding elegantly selfless, can never truly exist. And thankfully so. This is the type of thinking that lauds altruism and martyr-style parenting, never recognizing that no one can ever fully take themselves out of the relationship equation.

And thinking that I can serve someone else without any

motives of my own only increases the chances for my own self-deception and hidden expectations. You can see that ultimately this level of love always reverts to level 2, for I can never fully eliminate myself and my interests and my desires. Thankfully, we just weren't made that way. Again, we want relationships that involve others finding their own joy in being with us, pursuing their own happiness and ours. We do not want selfless martyrs living only for us—especially not a parent.

This brings us to Bernard's fourth and highest level of love, which he believed is the only way out of the either-me-or-you dilemma. Read this carefully, for this model of relating yourself to the world will probably sound unfamiliar and may even come across as heretical to your former way of thinking. But I believe it is the only way of relationship that makes any sense at all. Not only does it form the foundation of the entire ScreamFree philosophy, I believe it carries within it the power to create revolutionary relationships with our kids and everyone else in our world. Here goes:

Fourth Level of Love: "I love *me* for *your* benefit."
Read that heading again very carefully.

A person operating at this level says: "I love me, work on me, and build myself up so that I can come to you from a position of wholeness, a position of fullness. I take care of me so that you don't have to. From fullness I can then empty myself, my gifts, my love, my actions, for your ultimate benefit. I am the only one in charge of me, and I am the one ultimately responsible for me and my well-being. Therefore, as a steward of my greatest gift, my life, I need to take steps to ensure my health, my calmness of mind, my sanity, and my own validation as a person in the world. Thus, I can free you from having to provide those things for me. Thus, I can truly serve you without needing you to serve me."

Think of how this approach might radically change your relationships with your kids. You seek your own validation from within yourself so that regardless of how your children feel, behave, talk, or think, you are okay and are still committed to them. Think of the power in saying with all your actions "I take care of me so that you don't have to. I don't need you to appreciate me or validate me in order for me to still take care of you and of all of my responsibilities to you."

Loving yourself first is the only true way to be Scream-Free, because it is the only way to seek your own calm first. It is the only way to truly benefit your kids without burdening them with the need to benefit you. It is not their job—nor is it anyone else's—to meet your emotional and physical needs. As an adult, one who is responsible to so many others you love, it is up to you to pursue your own emotional fulfillment. This doesn't mean you don't ever need other people, not by a long shot. But it does mean that your life and your health are up to you. The sooner you embrace that truth and embrace the calling to love yourself first, the sooner you can truly serve all those around you, especially your kids.

Loving yourself first is the only true way to be ScreamFree, because it is the only way to seek your own calm first. It is the only way to truly benefit your kids without burdening them with the need to benefit you.

Our Cultural Confusion

I am aware that this vision of loving ourselves to benefit others offers a radical alternative for how to do relationships, especially for those of us in the West. This is because we in the West suffer a profound confusion about how to relate to ourselves. Perhaps the most profound example of this confusion occurs in our bellies.

So many Westerners suffer from obesity. In 2007, obesity is now America's number-one health crisis, especially in its effect on the economy. And although there is so much attention, funding, and research on the genetic components of being overweight, the diet and exercise industries are booming as well. This is because while people are overeating, they are starving for a way to take better care of themselves.

I believe that the major reason people are getting fatter and fatter, despite all the advancements in science and the proliferation of self-help materials, is that they are struggling with the very same false dichotomy we discussed earlier. For people to do all that is necessary to take better control of their weight and bodily health, they must learn to take better care of themselves. And to do that, people have to make intentional decisions to spend time, energy, and money focusing on themselves. Think about it. The only way to change your habits is to intentionally focus on yourself. But this idea runs counter to everything we've routinely believed about where our focus should be located. It's hard to take our focus off others, particularly our kids, when it feels like we're being terrible parents in order to do so.

Thus we end up apologizing for having to take time out to exercise! Or feeling guilty for wanting to get away, or not cooking a big dinner, or buying healthier food at the store.

While people are overeating, they are starving for a way to take better care of themselves.

I said earlier that other cultures do not seem to share our false dichotomy. The way the Hebrews and Jesus spoke, they already assumed a strong self-love. The Christian apostle Paul made the same assumption, at one point saying, "After all, no one ever hated his own body." This conclusion was logical at that time and in that culture.

But who do you know who doesn't hate his or her own body these days? Very few, I'm sure. Body image issues surround us so much that we cannot escape breathing in a culture of endless comparison and resulting self-hatred. Recently the Dalai Lama spoke about a conference he attended in the early 1990s of Western psychiatrists and psychologists discussing self-hatred. The Dalai Lama said that for the first hours of listening to these doctors, he thought his English was failing him. He asked himself and others, "Are they really saying 'self-hatred'?" He says he had never, in his vast experience of Eastern philosophy and politics, even considered the notion of self-hatred. But these doctors were speaking as if it were a very common, even epidemic, condition in the West. The Dalai Lama had no folder in his mind to categorize this human experience.

But we do. We know it all too well. And in one of the most futile moves possible, we hate how we feel about ourselves, and yet we try to use that hatred to motivate ourselves to change. Let's return to the weight issue. Fat Bastard, the obese Scotsman in the Austin Powers movies, summed it up this way: "I eat because I'm unhappy, and I'm unhappy because I eat. It's a vicious cycle."

As long as your motivation is your own self-loathing, there is no possible way to make a lasting positive change in your life. And the reason is simple. It's because the bad pattern you're trying to change, like overeating, is itself an attempt to make yourself feel better. So by trying to cut it out you are trying to cut out the only thing that makes you feel good. No wonder we sabotage our diets and exercise plans! As long as we're motivated by our self-hatred, then we'll never sustain any effort that feels like deprivation, hating ourselves more. Even if it's ultimately good for us.

This is because we don't feel or believe we have a legitimate right to treat ourselves well in the first place. Loving ourselves, and all the effort that takes, feels far too selfish or narcissistic.

But here's what is really selfish: sacrificing yourself for the sake of others while secretly needing them to validate and reciprocate your efforts in order to keep going. And narcissism is not focusing on yourself. Narcissism is needing everything and everyone else to focus on you.

In contrast, true self-love, the "I love me for your benefit" type of love, is always seeking to truly benefit others. The person who loves herself does not need others to recognize or even love her back in order to continue. Again, she takes care of herself so that others, particularly her kids, don't have to. And that is truly loving, both to yourself and others.

Putting on Your Own Oxygen Mask

What does loving yourself look like? Well, that depends on if you choose healthy ways or unhealthy ways to do it. How do you differentiate between healthy and unhealthy ways to treat yourself? Ask yourself one simple question: "Is this activity going to benefit both me and those I love?"

In order to flesh this out, let's look at the difference between an *escape* and a *retreat*. In the context of relationships, an escape is a purely selfish act. An escape is an unplanned action. It is often unintentional, and it is always done in haste. When you are attempting to escape from a situation, all you know is what you are running from—you honestly don't care to know what you're running to or why you're doing so. An escape is based on the need for self-preservation, and it hardly ever involves a plan of return. At its heart, an escape is simply another form of screaming. It is an anxiety-driven reaction, and it carries all the seeds for creating the very types of relationships we're hoping to avoid.

A retreat, however, is quite a different animal altogether. Retreats are intentional breaks from the action with the specific intent of regrouping and returning. In taking a retreat, you know where you are going and you know why you are going. You are retreating in order to benefit others as well as yourself. Retreats are a way to focus on yourself in order to become the best you imaginable. If you think this sounds selfish, consider this: Every great religious leader in history spent a significant amount of time in retreat before and/or during his or her service to the world. Consider Abraham,

Moses, Buddha, Jesus, Paul, Muhammad, Gandhi, Mother Teresa. I'd venture a guess that not one of these figures was ever called selfish. Heretical, yes. But never selfish.

Here's how escape and retreat are related: *The fewer intentional retreats we take for ourselves, the more we will find ourselves unintentionally finding ways to escape.* If we're not diligent in carving out retreats for ourselves in the form of healthy activities, we are sure to find an escape somewhere. Escapes for you may include obvious bad habits, such as smoking, overeating, or drinking to excess. You may find yourself getting completely lost in pornography, or romance novels, or fantasy lit. Or you may mentally or even physically "check out" of your family's life, pursuing an affair or just running away.

One way to lessen the likelihood of this desire to escape is to plan intentional retreats for yourself. Exercise, pamper yourself with a manicure, learn to play a musical instrument, meditate, seek personal growth. Pursue profoundly deep relationships with friends outside of your family. Take your spirituality to new heights, leaning on a higher power to provide you all the validation you need as a human being. Go after the employment or entrepreneurial endeavor you've always secretly craved but could never pursue openly.

You may be asking yourself "Who has the time?" You don't. That's just more evidence of the problem. You must *create* the time by choosing to put on your own oxygen mask first.

It is in the fabric of our culture, and it has been handed down to us generation after generation, that it is far better to deny ourselves, even hate ourselves, than it is to openly love ourselves first. A full discussion of our cultural difficulty with self-hatred and self-indulgence deserves its own book, and then some. For our purposes here, I want you to think of it in very practical terms for how to accept all your responsibility *to* your kids.

In an amazingly confessional interview near the end of his life, baseball great Mickey Mantle made a touching realization. In reflecting on his broken body and disintegrated relationships (especially as a father), the mighty Mick sighed, "If I knew I was going to live this long, I would have taken better care of myself."

How we live today determines so much of how we will live tomorrow. And how we live today and tomorrow determines so much about our relationships with our children.

I want you to think of it this way: *What has to last is what has to come first.*

YOUR HEALTH. A broken body makes it extremely difficult to provide for and protect your children. Your health is not an "extra" in your life, it is your first responsibility.

YOUR SELF-RESPECT. Compromising yourself by making empty threats, giving in to whining, and rescuing your kids from consequences is not a way to build long-term relationships. It is simply a way of devaluing yourself in your kids' eyes, and in your own. Learning to calm down and operate out of your principles is your calling as a parent, so safeguard and develop your self-respect with everything you have. Your grown children will thank you.

YOUR MARRIAGE. This is a another huge topic worthy of a book of its own, but know this: If you sacrifice your marriage for the sake of your kids, you will always, *always* end up sacrificing both.

Taking care of yourself for the sake of your kids is a life-long commitment. I hope this chapter has inspired you to make yourself a priority. You are so important to the world, beginning with your kids, that it is imperative that you take this teaching to heart.

So go take care of yourself; we deserve you at your best.

Reflection Questions

1. What is your initial, gut-level response to the idea of taking care of yourself for the benefit of others?

2. What are some ways you have neglected your own health—physical, emotional, mental, spiritual—for the sake of your kids?

3. What is the hardest part about taking care of yourself? What do you struggle with the most?

4. Describe the self-care habits you would need to develop in order to be at your best for others.

5. What commitment to your own care are you willing to make today?

CHAPTER TWELVE

Revolutionary Relationships

Don't you know?
They're talkin' about a revolution
It sounds like a whisper.
—Tracy Chapman, "Talkin' About a Revolution"

O f all the chapter title decisions in this book, "Revolutionary Relationships" was the most difficult to settle upon. The word "revolutionary" is thrown around so much that it often loses any meaning at all. It carries a number of applications and has found itself attached to a number of different expressions. From Marxist freedom fighters in third-world countries to the latest advancement in dishwasher detergent, "revolutionary" can describe almost anything.

What all these applications of the word "revolutionary" have in common, though, is the idea of a profound, effective, and lasting difference. A difference that changes our lives. Revolutions are turnarounds, upheavals, new starts. A revolution marks the beginning of the new, the creation of a reality we've only dreamed about. And I believe that's why you're reading this book. You want to turn around your relationships with your kids, creating new, lasting changes in your home. And that's why I wrote this. My passion is to share the principles I believe all parents need in order to create revolutions in their families. These are revolutions that forever change your days and weeks, your patterns and interactions, and the futures of your children and your children's children.

I used to employ the term "evolutionary" (without the "r") to describe the possibilities of ScreamFree Parenting. I liked that the term spoke of change, of process, of something new and different emerging as a possibility. What I learned, however, was that "evolutionary" carries with it a connotation connected to natural processes outside of our own conscious influence. Think evolution and you might think of the Big Bang theory of the origin of the universe, an event that simply happened outside of any personal intent. Well, that's not exactly what we're talking about here, is it?

We're talking about creating *r*evolutionary relationships, about making conscious choices to take hold of our own emotional reactions, taking responsibility for our own growth as parents. These are not processes outside of our influence; we are not simply going to wait for our relationships to improve! Most of us have tried that, and we've learned it puts us in the unenviable position of needing

everyone else to change. It doesn't work. In fact, such waiting on others has the remarkable tendency of helping to
create the type of relationships we all detest.

**We're talking about creating revolutionary
relationships, about making conscious choices
to take hold of our own emotional reactions.**

Parenting does carry with it all the possibilities of creating evolutionary changes within us and our relationships.
That is, there is a process larger than us working to trans-
form us and our relationships. But this process works only
if we have the courage to consciously take hold of ourselves
(and let go of others). This happens not by accident or natural happenstance, but by conscious choices you and I make
to curb our reactivity, calm our anxiety, and respond according to our principles.

Resistance to the Revolution

It is important to remember, though, that history never saw
a revolution without some form of resistance to it. And your
revolution will be no different, even as it is changing your
family for the better. Even terribly oppressive governments
have staunch supporters and citizens willing to die for
something that is clearly not intended to serve their best interests. Why? One simple word: familiarity.

When we engage in relationships, at any level, we function in a pattern with the other person—a dance, if you will. You've heard the phrase "It takes two to tango." The same is true for relationships. Each year, my wife begins her school year teaching a play by Henrik Ibsen, the noted Norwegian author. This play, titled *A Doll's House*, examines the marriage relationship between the two main characters, Nora and Torvald Helmer. Nora is an irritating, childlike, manipulative woman who behaves in extremely immature ways. Torvald is an overbearing and harsh husband who treats his wife like an object. Nora sneaks cookies and hides money from Torvald. Torvald calls Nora only by pet names and often demeans her with insults. When my wife's students discuss these characters, they often are quick to blame one character or the other for the faulty relationship. The comments usually go something like this:

"Nora is so annoying! I can't stand the way she's always dancing around the house acting like she's fourteen. No wonder Torvald treats her like a kid . . . she *is* one!"

"No way! The only reason she acts that way is because of the way he treats her. He never talks to her about anything important and he's always calling her 'my little squirrel'— and 'my pet'—puke. I don't blame her for acting selfish; he certainly doesn't seem to care about her."

Well, they're both right. Nora and Torvald are in a dance. He treats her like a child, so she acts like one. She acts like a child, so he treats her as one. Trying to figure out who started the pattern is about as fruitful as discussing which came first, the chicken or the egg, or discussing which horse is the first one on a carousel. No one "started it." And besides, it doesn't matter. What does matter is the fact that the pattern is strong. Is it strong because both participants like the way in which it serves them? No. Its strength lies in its familiarity.

We are more comfortable with the known—even in misery—than we are with the unknown. Patterns are so powerful because they provide stability, even if that stability is wretched. So it's no wonder that when one person attempts to step out of the dance and change the pattern, he or she will encounter strong resistance.

We are more comfortable in the known—even in misery—than we are in the unknown.

When you start your ScreamFree revolution in your home, your children (and maybe even your spouse) will pull out all the stops to lure you back into the old dance. This is not a conscious or intentional effort on their part. And even though it may feel malicious or manipulative, trust me, it is not. It is merely a mechanism for their own survival in the family. They want things to go back to "normal," even if they hated "normal" in the first place.

But you are learning to grow yourself up, and as you grow, you are able to tolerate such efforts to pull you down. A client recently told me that after an extended period of practicing ScreamFree Parenting, her thirteen-year-old finally had enough.

"I hate it when you're calm!" she screamed.

Know this: If you're getting that type of response, you are building the immeasurable type of mutual respect in your home that creates and maintains revolutionary relationships. All you have to do is stay the course: Focus on yourself, calm yourself down, and grow yourself up. You will be amazed at your ability to not only implement the changes you want to make, but to also withstand any resistance to your efforts. And you will be amazed at what happens in your family when you do.

The Trying Threes

We are now coming to the end of the book. In an effort to keep you inspired as you begin your revolutionary journey, I want to tell you one more success story. This story takes us into that stressful phase reserved for parents and their toddlers, but with a few simple adjustments it could just as easily be a story about adolescents or teens, with whom we can dance in ways that are every bit as stressful and demanding. My coaching client Steve recently told me of an encounter with his three-year-old that well illustrates the possibilities of ScreamFree Parenting. As you read about it, look for the test provided for Steve's growth in this fairly typical situation (bedtime with a three-year-old). Then look even closer for the revolution Steve's creating from the inside out by consciously deciding to stay both calm and connected.

Having recently moved across the country in order for his wife to return to work, Steve's family had seen an enormous amount of transition as of late. Everyone in the family seemed stressed, as each had to adjust to new schedules, roles, and tasks. One Sunday evening, Steve's wife had to go to the office. It was thus his job to put their three-year-old daughter, Sarah, to bed. With all the changes in the previous weeks, bedtimes had not been easy.

When faced with the chore of cleaning up her toys, Sarah moved into her most skillful stall tactics: acting too tired; talking in a cute baby voice; and so on. With incredible resolve, Steve refused to become reactive. He also refused to leave the scene.

As Sarah began to talk rudely to Steve, he calmly asked her, "What do you think will happen if you do that again?"

They both agreed that the consequence would be a time-out. Steve gave Sarah the clear option of cleaning up or having a time-out. She chose to continue stalling. Steve calmly brought in her time-out chair and placed it in her room. Again he gave her the clear choice. Sarah stalled and Steve resolutely put her in her chair. Sarah cried out, kicking and screaming. Steve offered to sit next to her, but she refused. She became adamant against cleaning up, so Steve proceeded to tell her of the next consequences.

The bright three-year-old knew this involved putting one or more of her movies into timeout for a day, so she ran down to stand in front of the entertainment center, wanting to protect them. She assumed the stance of a hockey goalie, aiming to block any of Steve's attempts to get past her. Steve somehow managed to contain both his anger and his laughter at the situation, and calmly explained that Sarah really could protect her videos by choosing to clean up. Upon her repeated refusal, he then deftly managed to slip past her and pull out one of the movies.

Hysterical by then, Sarah grabbed for the movie, then ran to the couch, screaming, obviously tired, still refusing to clean up. Again Steve stated her choices very clearly, and then she did something different. She now said she wanted Mommy. Here Steve faced his most difficult choice of all. He could have chosen to take such a statement personally, receiving it as an indictment of him as a parent. He could have reacted another way, choosing to force Sarah into compliance. Instead, he chose the moment as a window of opportunity to grow closer to his child. This would be a real test, one that challenged him but promised him great rewards for his efforts.

Steve sat beside Sarah on the couch, embraced her, and created some emotional space for them both. Sarah cried out that Mommy wasn't supposed to go to work at night; it was too dark. She wanted her mommy back home.

Steve chose to hear his daughter's plea: "It's one thing for Mommy to go to work during the day, but she's supposed to be home when it's dark," he empathized. The recent transitions were taking their toll on a three-year-old's heart. Steve went with the momentum, saying "Yeah, I miss Mommy too. She needed some special time for herself tonight, and that's okay. But I miss her too."

The two embraced for a moment or two, with Sarah beginning to calm herself and quiet her tears. Steve then offered to share a bedtime snack with her and talk about Mommy. He asked what she missed most about her mother. Sarah explained that she liked it when her mother is home at bedtime and chooses to "lay with me" in her bed. Steve agreed that those are special times and reiterated that while it was okay for Mommy to be gone, he missed her too. (He couldn't help but think about how many nights his wife had had to say those same words on his behalf.) They enjoyed their bedtime snack, with Steve setting his watch alarm to go off after a few minutes. This would remind them both that bedtime, and cleaning up the living room, still awaited.

When the watch beeped, Sarah was the one who said it was time to go clean up. Perhaps Steve's hard work was paying off. She proceeded to put away her books and toys as Steve got her toothbrush ready and praised Sarah for her efforts to clean up. He even helped a little. Sarah then tried to go potty; again Steve praised her for the effort.

Once in bed, Sarah asked Steve for a story, and he spun one of his classics. As Sarah's eyes began to droop, Steve rose to leave, only to be hailed back with a special invitation: "Daddy, would you lay with me?"

Steve gladly accepted the request. As if that were not rewarding enough, however, he then experienced one of those rare moments that occasionally rewards the hard work of ScreamFree Parenting. Sarah looked into his eyes and explained, "I still miss Mommy."

Choosing to remain nonreactive and to go with the momentum, Steve replied, "I know, sweetheart. I miss her too."

Sarah then ended their dialogue with the invitation we all long for: "Daddy, would you come closer?" He drew closer and began to stroke her hair. Sleep came only a few moments later.

As Steve left the room, he knew his hard work had paid off. He had not simply held his ground in the battle of attrition, as most of us try to do with our parenting. Steve had actually risen above the battle altogether. He had actually used a stress-filled time as an opportunity for growth and had walked away with the invitation any parent would love to receive: "Daddy, would you come closer?"

The Revolution We All Wish For

Those words Steve heard that night are revolutionary words, especially because they came not from a manipulated and needy little girl, but from the genuine wishes of a begrudgingly respectful human being.

And isn't that what we all crave in our relationships? Someone to authentically invite us closer? Isn't that the longing behind every human relationship? That someone would choose to be with us, not because we had to coerce or trick or beg them, but because they genuinely wanted to?

Think back to your own childhood years. Even then you knew what you really wanted: Someone who wanted you. Remember asking Mommy or Daddy why they loved you? Was it simply because they had to? You wanted to know you were inherently lovable, outside of some blood obligation. You wanted to know your mom *chose* to love you; that your dad *wanted* to be close to you. That desire hasn't gone away.

That's what we all still want most in the world, from all of our relationships: freely chosen love. And that's what we want most from and for our kids. We crave a relationship with each of our kids that springs from respect and their authentic choice, not from our heavy-handed or passive-aggressive manipulation. We also crave relationships *for* our kids that are models of respect and mutually chosen love. And that's revolutionary.

I firmly believe that a revolutionary relationship with each of our kids is possible for each and every one of us. And that means you. Regardless of your children's ages and regardless of your past mistakes, such revolutionary relationships are possible for you.

Of course, the irony is that to grasp that type of revolution, you have to let go. It takes courage, but you must let go of your child's reactions, you must let go of your child's emotions, and you must let go of your child's choices. What you must grasp in order to start a revolution are your own reactions, your own emotions, your own choices. "If you love them, set them free" is only half of the equation. The real key is learning to take hold of all the responsibility it takes to be you.

You are not responsible *for* your kids, their behavior, their feelings, or any of their choices. You are responsible *to* them for your behavior, your feelings, and all of your choices. And every time you grasp that reality, you are indeed creating a revolution in your life and in the world.

It All Begins with One Sentence

Every revolution, no matter how large or small, always begins with one sentence. Every significant change to a system, whether it be a society, a nation, a company, or even a family like yours, always begins with the same communicated message:

"I'm not sure what anyone else is going to do, but this is what I'm going to do."

Revolutions don't start with loud, bold proclamations. Life-altering changes do not begin with gangs of people all simultaneously acting as one. They begin with quiet statements, quiet actions of singular fortitude. They begin with a singular individual with a resounding resolve to change herself, whatever the outcome.

I was not fully aware of this until a world-mover passed away in 2005, a world-mover who refused to move.

Like most of us, Rosa Parks did not see herself as a revolutionary. Yes, she was involved in the local chapter of the NAACP, and thus she was involved in the burgeoning civil rights movement. But she was also a wife and a seamstress, living in the segregated South of the 1950s. Once, when asked about the atmosphere of her home city of Montgomery, she replied that things would never be different because the black community "could never come together." And yet one day she decided to ignore that lack of solidarity. She decided on her own, as an individual, to do something different.

Making the changes we want in our lives, in our relationships, always begins by simply doing something different. This reflects an awareness that all behavior comes couched in a pattern, the "dance" I spoke of earlier. Because this dance exists, you can predict how your son is going to stall at bedtime. Or what your daughter is going to say when you tell her to clean her room. These are patterns, and just as much as you can pinpoint your children's parts in the pattern, they can pinpoint yours.

And as you've read throughout this book, the only way to change the pattern is to focus on your own part in it, and then do something different. That's what Rosa Parks did. She knew that as long as she waited for other people to change, whether it be the white community in power or the black community by struggling to unite, she was in a helpless position. But if she herself, with or without anyone else's cooperation, did something different . . .

In December 1955, Rosa Parks left work and went to the bus stop. It was time to go home, and she was tired. When the bus stopped to pick her up, she did as she always had: She entered through the front door, paid the bus fare, then went back out of the bus and reentered through the back door, the "Colored" entrance. Mrs. Parks then proceeded to take a seat on the fifth row, which was the first row of the "Colored" section. Then the bus began to move.

Over the course of more stops, the bus started to fill up. Before it reached Mrs. Parks's stop, the bus was completely full. That meant her fifth row was filled, with two African Americans on the right side and two across the aisle on the left. Then, at the next stop, a white man entered through the front door. There were no seats available in the first four rows (they were all taken up by white people), so the man, as was customary, went to sit in the fifth row.

Now, the segregation laws of the time stated that persons of color were forbidden to: (a) sit in the white section; (b) share a seat in the "Colored" section next to a white person; or (c) sit across the aisle from a white person.

This meant that when the white man moved to sit in the full fifth row, all four persons of color had to get up, by law, and stand in the back of the bus.

Three of them did. Rosa Parks, calmly, did not.

Mrs. Parks did not intend to be a hero. She just did not want to continue her part of the pattern. She did not want to give up her seat. And she absolutely would not budge. She would later say that she "felt a wave of determination fall over me like a blanket." She made no loud protests, she issued no bold demands. According to witnesses, she didn't even make an upset face or a frown. She did not ask anyone else to change for her sake; she simply refused to move.

And when the bus driver informed her that he would have to have her arrested, Rosa Parks uttered her version of that one sentence that starts every significant change: "Then you go ahead and do what you need to do. But I'm not moving."

And the rest is glorious history. Her trial and conviction led a twenty-six-year-old minister from Atlanta to organize a 381-day bus boycott, crippling the local transportation industry and creating a national civil rights movement. A true revolution.

In this book, I make a promise that you can, indeed, start a revolution in your home. I sometimes hesitate to use that language because I would never want to cheapen the memory and inspiration of true revolutionaries like Rosa Parks and Dr. Martin Luther King, Jr.

But what we're talking about here is bringing to a similar end the destructive patterns that have driven some families for generations. What we're talking about here is creating new patterns of influence and intimacy that can transcend the reactionary dialogues and messages that fill our brainwaves (and airwaves).

What we're talking about is learning to create the relationships we've always craved, by simply learning to focus on ourselves, calm ourselves down, and grow ourselves up.

"I'm not sure what anyone else is going to do, but this is what I'm going to do."

Now it's up to you.

Reflection Questions

1. What do you think of when you hear the word "revolutionary"?

2. What type of resistance do you think you might encounter as you begin to change yourself?

3. What is one ScreamFree principle you can focus on this week? How might you go about practicing that principle today?

4. What type of relationship environment do you want to create in your home? Describe each relationship and what patterns you would like to change in order to revolutionize it.

5. What is one pattern you would like to end? What is your part of that pattern? What is one thing you could do differently, even without the cooperation or support of anyone else, that would change that pattern today?

ACKNOWLEDGMENTS

At times during the writing of this book I doubted whether I would ever get to write this part. Amazingly, here I am. And of course, like every other author before and after me, I must acknowledge that writing is a team effort.

Such is *ScreamFree Parenting*. I started this dream way back during my family therapy internship many years ago and, thanks to so very many along the way, this book, and the company launching it, ScreamFree Living, Incorporated, is now a solid and growing reality.

The one constant team member along the entire journey is the one to whom this book is dedicated—my wife of thirteen years, Jenny. She is the best friend, spouse, or parent I know, or know of. But that does not begin to acknowledge her giftedness, loyalty, support, patience, and love for me and this project. I consider her nothing less than co-creator of this material, for she has learned the principles along with me, she practices the principles better than I do, and she holds me to the principles whenever I let my anxiety get the better of me. She is an amazing co-parent, co-creator, and collaborator and I cannot thank her enough for her editing, writing, encouragement, vision, and undaunted courage.

The team along the way has grown, but three in particular deserve special mention:

FRITZ MILLER, along with the support of his wife, Tami, has been with me from the very beginning. Besides his obvious graphic design and marketing talents, Fritz demonstrates an amazingly honest and encouraging spirit. Fritz, I consider you one of my closest friends, and your belief in me helps keep me going.

DAVE MARKERT, along with the support of his wife, Dorothy, has shown a pure passion for the ScreamFree vision since he first heard me present it at a conference in 2003. Not only has he worked diligently to instill the principles into his own life and family, but also he has jumped in headfirst to help launch this company into the world. Dave, you are a brilliant marketer, an inspiring leader, and a wonderful partner. And my brother in every way but blood.

JON KAPLAN, along with the support of his wife Tasha, came on board a little later than the others, but in no time became a full partner in the endeavor. He has a remarkable business mind and sales passion, giving us new visions of how far we can take the ScreamFree message. He has also brought a strong passion for family and friendship. Jon, you are my brother and friend, and one of my favorite activities in the world is dreaming about the future with you over a glass of cabernet.

Since the initial launch of the company a couple of years ago, a few others have joined our little band and are now integral parts of the family:

TERESA MYER, along with the support of her husband,

Mike, has brought technological expertise, faithful vision, and a wonderful wit to the project—which any woman would need working alongside all of us obnoxious men. I hope you feel welcome, Teresa.

TERRY CHASTAIN, along with the support of his wife, Lynn, shares a similar wit, and he's brought a newfound organization to our coaching and training programs. Terry and Lynn, your obvious belief in me and this message has already led to some amazing connections and new directions. Thank you.

Some special, supportive friends deserve mention next:

CHARLIE ANDERSON, whose boundless wisdom and abounding faith is fuel for this mission. Charlie, I'm loving the development of our friendship as well. And for all of this I have to especially thank your wife, Julie, for reading, recommending, and readily supporting this whole endeavor. Thank you both for your blatant love for me, my family, and this company.

DON and BRENDA CARROLL, your outstanding provision and support have literally started and kept us going. We love your enthusiasm and your generosity, and, of course, your taste in food. Let's look forward to more celebrations at Fogo's! (And you're not too shabby as grandparents, Mom and Don—thank you so much.)

FERNANDO NASMYTH has been with me this whole way. He has shown the utmost respect for my dreams and has never shrugged off my vision for us to work together. Thank you, Fernando, for all of your support of me and my family since welcoming us to Atlanta seven years ago.

The same goes for David Blackwell, Dane Booth, and John Turner. Thank you for your friendship, boys, and may

Monday nights continue to celebrate more than just football.

I also want to give thanks to Roger Herring, my accountant, and Don Sloane, my personal and professional coach. Roger, you are an excellent entreprenuer, gifted thinker, and a huge support to me since the beginning. Don, you have helped me more than you know (but you hear that from all your clients!). Your encouragement, wisdom, and yes, love, have inspired me to this point. I'll see you backstage!

Two of my mentors deserve special mention: Drs. Joe Whitwell and Kerry Duncan. You both have nurtured my growth as a therapist, and I thank you for believing in me. I thank you all the more, however, for nurturing me as a man.

There are several who have actually helped with the writing of this book. Struggling to turn thoughts into pages, I leaned heavily on these gifted writers and editors to produce the best work possible. Of course, any errors belong to me, not them.

JOHN TURNER, a gifted writer, thinker, and family man, helped launch the book by completing the first chapter and working on several others as well. There are phrases throughout the book that come from his ingenuity, and I am grateful. I am also grateful for his initial enthusiasm and continued encouragement, reminding me how truly revolutionary this material is.

KIM DIEHL, another gifted writer and editor, also helped me craft a number of the chapters, lending both her writing skills and her parenting experience to the manuscript. Kim, you were wonderful during a needy time. Thank you.

ANGIE FANN also helped tremendously in editing and finishing the project. Angie, you were here when I needed you and you showed me more talent than I think I knew you had.

My mother, Brenda Carroll, was also very gifted and generous in her proofreading and editing. Thanks so much, Mom!

And here I must again thank Jenny, who deserves credit for at least five chapters finding their completion, with each ending up better than I thought possible. Jenny, your history professor was right all those years ago: You need to keep writing.

I could not have arrived at this point as a thinker, therapist, or author without the sound theoretical and clinical base of Bowen Family Systems Theory. Dr. Murray Bowen is the most underrated thinker of the twentieth century and his thought and practice are finally beginning to receive their due. It is my professional mission to translate Bowen's systems thinking into the working dialogue of families and organizations around the world. I am thankful to all those who have introduced me to and instructed me in this way of thinking, living, and working with relationships. These include Drs. Waymon Hinson, Jackie Halstead and Tom Milholland of Abilene Christian University, which is, in my estimation, the finest marriage and family therapy training facility in the country. I am especially thankful to Dr. Major Boglin, now in Atlanta, who has directly instructed me in Bowen's thought and practice more than anyone. And, of course, I am ever grateful to those who have come after Dr. Bowen, faithfully interpreting his work as they develop their own. The world is grateful to Drs. Edwin Friedman, David Schnarch, Roberta Gilbert, Harriet Lerner, and

Michael Kerr, to name a few. *ScreamFree Parenting* may not look like it at first glance, but it is my first attempt to build upon your work.

To all of my therapy, coaching, and consulting clients, I give my heartfelt thanks for allowing me into your lives. Opening yourselves up and confessing your "I don't know"s to anyone is the most courageous act on earth, and I am honored to have been the recipient of that privilege. Your lives have inspired me as a person, and your stories throughout this book (although changed dramatically to protect your confidentiality) will inspire countless others. To all of those who have attended my seminars, thank you for your energy, your feedback, and your continued success as you revolutionize your relationships.

There have been so many believers, ambassadors, and investors so far that I feel tremendously overwhelmed. These include: Don and Brenda Carroll, Dave Cormack, Steven H. King, Frances Carden, Ken Runkel, Molly Faulk, George Miller, Greg and Gwen Duriez, Fred and Charlotte Miller, Fernando Nasmyth, Jeff and Suzie Parrow, Mary Sada, Christopher and Sheila Stilitto, June and Scotty Witt, and Shane and Leah Bowen. Thank you all for your willingness to risk. I am responsible to you for the rest of the way.

Thanks so much to my and Jenny's extended families. Your support throughout our marriage has been superlative, and your overt excitement about this project has gone so far to make it possible.

Finally, there have been a few people who have literally led me from being a therapist with a book idea to an author with a burgeoning franchise.

MEG LABORDE and everyone else at Greenleaf Book

Group immediately loved the manuscript and then gave us the distribution we so desperately craved (and needed) as self-publishers.

BILL THOMAS and TRICIA MEDVED at Broadway Books obviously loved the book as well, and the marketing vision behind it, or they would have never risked so much to bring it to life. Thank you.

STACY CREAMER, my editor and our "screamer" at Broadway Books and Random House, has provided outstanding leadership into the world of big publishing. Stacy, I'm loving our developing relationship and look forward to arguing over many manuscripts to come.

And finally and wonderfully, I thank Dena Fischer of Manus & Associates Literary Agency, Inc., for begging to represent me as my agent (just kidding). From our initial conversations to our celebratory dinners, I have loved having you in my life. I light up when I see you on caller ID, and I cannot wait to see how many mutual congratulations we share over the next ten years and beyond.

NOTES

PART 1

1. E. H. Friedman, *Friedman's Fables* (New York: Guilford Press, 1990).

Chapter 2

1. Jamie B. Raser, *Raising Children You Can Live With: A Guide for Frustrated Parents* (Houston: Bayou Publishing, 1999), p. 13.

Chapter 3

1. David Schnarch, *Passionate Marriage: Keeping Love and Intimacy Alive in Committed Relationships* (New York: Owl Books, 1998).

PART 2

Chapter 5

1. Dallas Willard, *The Divine Conspiracy: Rediscovering Our Hidden Life in God* (San Francisco: HarperSanFrancisco, 1998), p. 21.
2. Scott Turansky and Joanne Miller, *Good and Angry: Exchanging Frustration for Character . . . in You and Your Kids!* (Colorado Springs, CO: Shaw Books, 2002), pp. 136–137.

Chapter 6

1. Kano, Jigoro, "Judo: The Japanese Art of Self-Defense," The Original Judo Information Site, http://www.judoinfo.com/kano2.html (accessed October 30, 2004).
2. Ibid.

PART 3

Chapter 8

1. Jamie B. Raser, *Raising Children You Can Live With: A Guide for Frustrated Parents* (Houston: Bayou Publishing, 1999), pp. 14–17.
2. John Friel and Linda Friel, *The Seven Worst Things (Good) Parents Do* (Deerfield Beach, FL: HCI, 1999), pp. 84–85.

Chapter 9

1. Roger Allen and Ron Rose, *Common Sense Discipline* (Colorado Springs, CO: David C. Cook Publishers, 2001).

PART 4

Chapter 11

1. Taken from Bernard of Clairvaux, *On Loving God*. Can be viewed at http://www.ccel.org/ccel/bernard/loving_god.html.
2. I am extremely grateful to Dr. Carrol Osburn of Abilene Christian University for this interpretation of Bernard's work.

More ScreamFree Parenting!

You can listen in on author and speaker Hal Runkel as he presents his revolutionary screamfree message to a live audience of parents. This seminar offers **additional stories** and breakthrough insights presented in Hal's unique and engaging manner. Each DVD or Audio CD contains **questions and answers** from real parents with **actual parenting issues**. Lively, energetic, and often humorous, Hal interacts with the audience in a way that will give you valuable tools to help you create the relationships you've always craved.

Seminar on DVD, CD Audio, or online podcast.

See free clips at www.screamfree.com/dvd

Join the international movement of parents who are revolutionizing relationships with their kids.

Visit **www.screamfree.com** today!